365

OUTDOOR

Activities

Contributing Writers
Maria Birmingham
Karen E. Bledsoe
Kelly Milner Halls

Illustrations
Anne Kennedy

Publications International, Ltd.

Maria Birmingham is the managing editor for *OWL* magazine, a children's science and nature publication in Canada. She has also contributed to *Chickadee* magazine and freelances on other children's projects.

Karen E. Bledsoe is a member of the Society of Children's Book Writers and Illustrators. She is the author of *Pocketful of Memories: School Days,* co-author of *365 Nature Crafts,* and has written other fiction for adults and children. Karen has worked as an environmental educator, recreational leader, teacher, and college instructor.

Kelly Milner Halls is a freelance writer whose work frequently appears in *Highlights for Children, Guideposts for Kids, Freezone, Boys' Life, Fox Kids* and the *Chicago Tribune.* Her books include *Dino-Trekking* and *I Bought a Baby Chicken.* She is also the co-author of *365 After School Activities.*

Illustrations: Anne Kennedy

Contents

Enjoying the Great Outdoors

AH, THE GREAT OUTDOORS! From remote mountaintops to your own backyard, the outdoors offer unlimited opportunity for exploration, discovery, learning, and fun. Have you ever sat among the tall firs and listened to the whistling wind? Or watched wild birds as they gather around a feeder? Tried to track all the bugs in your neighborhood? Or followed a trail through the woods, wondering what surprises lay around the next bend? Are the words *camping, hiking,* and *picnics* your magic words?

If so, then let this book be your guide to outdoor fun and learning. Follow the great explorers as you travel (by car or by foot), camp overnight, and cook over a fire. Learn as the famous naturalists did when you make your own observations on nature and conduct your own experiments. Get fit and have fun with outdoor games. Express yourself as you make unique art with natural materials.

Remember, though, that our natural resources are for everyone to share. Those who explore nature must leave it for others to enjoy. On hikes and campouts, practice "leave no trace" techniques. Erase all signs of your campsite when you leave. Pick up trash that others may have left and leave your campsite or trail better than you found it.

Hike only on established trails. Going off-trail causes erosion and increases your chances of getting lost. Know and obey the rules and regulations of public lands. When observing wild animals, be careful not to disturb them, especially when they're nesting. Never, *ever* shoot or throw rocks at animals. Observe animals from a safe distance, and remember that all animals may bite, claw, kick, or peck you if they feel threatened.

And never feed wild animals! Snack foods aren't good for them, and hand-feeding wild animals can cause them to overpopulate while people are around. The animals then starve to death when tourist season is over.

Leave plants for others to enjoy. Wildflowers are more beautiful growing free in meadows than when stuffed in a vase. Take photos if you want to enjoy their beauty.

In addition, be safe. Nature isn't an amusement park! There are no safety belts or equipment inspections; use common sense and be alert for all hazards. Stay away from the edges of cliffs and rocky shorelines. Watch large animals from a safe distance. Wear flotation devices when boating or when you are around deep water. Know what poisonous plants and reptiles live in the area you're going into. Always take a responsible adult with you when you explore. Stay with your group when you are hiking, and use maps so you don't get lost. Carry extra food and water. Before drinking from an outdoor source, be sure to boil the water.

Even around where you live, caution is the word. Watch out for garbage or loose toys on the lawn when you're playing outside. Never stay outside if it gets too hot or too cold—you're better off in the house.

In these activities, notice the number of leaves by each title. One leaf indicates an easy project, two are for projects that are a bit harder, and three indicate a more challenging project. You should be able to do all the projects with one leaf and most of the projects with two leaves all by yourself. Ask an adult for advice when you tackle a project with three leaves. Watch also for warnings about hazards. Some projects may require the use of stoves, sharp blades, or flames. Get an adult to help you with these.

Many of these projects will require you to ask an adult for permission. You'll want to know if all the materials you need are available in your house for you to use. Adults can also help you get materials you don't have at home. Better yet, adults may have ideas to make your project even more fun. Once you pick an activity or project, read the instructions carefully so you know exactly what to do. Be sure you have the materials and time you need. Most activities require only simple household items, but a few may require a trip to the store.

Plants, Trees, and Seeds

From a tiny seed can grow an enormous tree or a gorgeous flower. How does it happen? Discover the mysteries hidden in seeds, flowers, and plants with the activities in this chapter. Go outdoors to enjoy the wonders of trees. Try some of the gardening activities to grow flowers of your own and use them to make lovely art projects. Or turn your garden into a fun place to play by growing a bean teepee or a sunflower fort. Let's get growing!

Sunflower Fort

Grow your own leafy playhouse!

What You'll Need:
7' x 7' garden patch, shovel, short stakes, string, tall-growing sunflower seeds (such as giant greystripe or Russian mammoth), cheesecloth (optional)

LATE IN SPRING, when the weather is warm, mark a seven-foot square in the garden. Dig the ground around the edges a foot deep. The soil should be loose and crumbly. Push a stake in the ground at each corner. Mark the "doorway" with stakes. To help you plant seeds in straight lines, tie string to a doorway stake and run the string around the stakes in a square around your fort. Plant seeds an inch deep and six inches apart. (Poke a hole in the dirt with your finger, put a seed in, and cover it up.) Plant seeds around the edges of your fort—but not the doorway. Water the seeds.

Cover the seeds with a layer of cheesecloth to protect them from squirrels. Leave the cloth loose so the plants can grow; weigh down the edges with dirt. When the plants are several inches tall, remove the cheesecloth. Thin out the plants; sunflowers get huge and need the room. Keep the plants watered, as sunflowers need plenty of moisture.

By the Letter

Spell it out—the green thumb way.

What You'll Need:
Small section of soil,
quick-sprouting
seeds,
water

EVERYONE LIKES to express their own personal style. So why not let your garden speak for itself? The next time you plant quick-sprouting seeds (ask your local outdoor gardening clerk which seeds sprout fastest in your geographic area), spell out just how you feel. Plant in the shape of the first letter of your name, your favorite sports team, or even your favorite singer. Take it a step further and plant only seeds that will bloom in your favorite colors. It'll be a garden all your own.

Sun Jam

Make delicious strawberry preserves using the heat of the sun.

What You'll Need:
One quart of ripe
strawberries (small
berries rather than
large ones), safe
knife, ten-inch
saucepan, four cups
of sugar, large
spoon, large glass
baking dish,
clear plastic wrap,
container

MAKE THIS JAM when the weather will be hot and sunny for several days. Cut your washed berries in half and put them in a saucepan. Add the sugar, stir, and let the pan sit 30 minutes. With adult help, heat the mixture on the stove medium-high until it boils. Turn the heat to low and simmer 15 minutes.

Next, with adult help, pour the hot mix into a glass baking dish. Let it cool 15 minutes, then cover the pan in plastic wrap. Leave the pan in the sun all day. Stir the berries gently two or three times during the day. Bring the pan inside at night. It will take two or three days for the mixture to thicken. When the preserves are ready, store them in the refrigerator. Sometimes this recipe works, sometimes it doesn't—every batch is different. If your preserves don't jell, use them for strawberry syrup!

Popcorn Plants

No butter is required when you grow this popcorn garden!

What You'll Need:
Paper towels,
plastic bag that zips
shut, water,
unpopped kernels
of popcorn,
tape,
planter pot, soil

WE KNOW that popcorn makes a great snack at the movies. It can also be turned into a plant. When you're ready to get popping, put a few paper towels in a plastic bag and soak them with water. Now place a few popcorn kernels in the bag so they sit on top of the paper towels. Zip the bag up and tape it to an object (like a fence) where it can get plenty of sunlight.

Keep an eye on the kernels over the next week or two. If the towels dry up, pour some more water into the bag until the towels soak it up.

Once you see small plants growing, place them in a pot filled with soil. Keep the soil moist and watch your popcorn plants reach for the sky!

Carve it Out

Make your mark with a pumpkin.

What You'll Need:
Sunny garden spot,
dwarf pumpkin
seeds or starts,
water,
clean nail

WHEN YOU GROW your very own dwarf pumpkin, there's a way to make it reflect your personal moods. All it takes is a clean nail. Plant dwarf pumpkin seeds or starts in a sunny spot in your garden. After they grow from seeds to flowers to melons, and when they are yellow and just about to turn orange, carve your name in the skin of the pumpkin with a clean, sharp nail. (Be careful not to slip and "nail" your own skin.) As the pumpkin continues to grow, the skin will scar over your marks, leaving a very personal signature.

Grow a Garden

Put your green thumb to work and grow plants from scratch!

What You'll Need:

Seeds from fruit (like apples, oranges, grapefruit, lemons, or limes), dish of water, plant pot, soil

READY TO MAKE your own home-grown plants? A few days before you start your garden, you might want to ask your family to save the seeds they find in any fruit that they eat. You can do the same with the fruit you gobble down. That way, when you're ready to grow, you'll have plenty of seeds to use.

Once you have eight to ten fruit seeds, fill a small dish with water and soak the seeds for a day or two. Then fill a plant pot with soil. Bury the seeds about a quarter of an inch deep in the soil and water them. Over the next few weeks, watch your seeds carefully. Keep the plant pot in a sunny place and water the seeds every couple of days. Soon you'll see plants pop through the soil.

The Lowdown on Dirt

When it comes to supporting plant life, not all dirt is equal.

What You'll Need:

Garden soil, trowel, small flowerpots with saucers, water, bean seeds, tall stakes, pencil or pen, ruler, paper (graph paper optional), tape

LOOK IN YOUR YARD for areas where plants grow poorly. Is the soil trampled and hard? Is the soil soft and loose where plants grow well? Look for sandy or heavy, clay-like soil. Gather samples of different soils and fill a flowerpot with each kind.

Label your flowerpots: "Hard, baked soil near the sidewalk," "Loose, fluffy soil from the flower bed," etc. Water the pots, then plant two or three bean seeds in each. Put a stake in each pot for the beans to climb. Keep the pots moist (but not soggy) while the beans sprout. Notice which beans sprout first. Measure the height of the plants every few days until the beans flower. Keep a chart. Which soil was the best?

A Garden of Good Scents

Grow sweet-smelling plants that delight the nose and the eyes.

What You'll Need:

Patch of sunny ground about five feet wide and six feet long (get permission first), shovel, trowel, bagged compost, bagged bark mulch, plants, hose, small sprinkler, cardboard, safe scissors, marker

CHOOSE A GARDEN spot and prepare the soil as noted in "Sunny Flower Garden" (page 29). Then, make two paths by pressing down a one-foot wide strip of soil down the middle of the garden and a second one going across. Cover the paths with bark mulch about two inches deep. Buy your plants or seeds at a garden center.

Set the plants out and arrange them the way you wish. Use the labels in the pots to help you decide where to place them. Sow seeds according to the directions on the package. When everything is planted, run a sprinkler about a half an hour. Water deeply twice a week during dry weather and pull out weeds often.

When your garden is ready, make a sign that says "Please Touch the Plants!" Then invite friends inside. Some plants that release scents when touched are Sweet Alyssum, Heliotrope, Nasturtium, Scented Geraniums, Basil, English Violets, Lavender, Pinks, Thyme, Sage, and Oregano.

In the Garden

Although lawns and gardens have a long history, modern lawns became popular only after 1832, when the push mower was invented. Before then, lawns were cut by teams of men with scythes—or by sheep!

Jack (or Joan or Jim or Judy) & the Beanstalk

Magic (even without those magic beans).

What You'll Need:

Garden spot, three equal-length dowel rods or branches, pole bean seeds, water, plastic villagers or army men

FICTION BECOMES fact—almost—thanks to this fantasy garden plot complete with little plastic figures. The next time you plant pole beans (the "reach for the stars" vines that crawl way up stakes and fences), set up a tiny village too. Arrange plastic people at the base of the plant and the pole you stake down for it to climb. Before you know it, your fantasy folk will be settled around a gigantic adventure. You'll grow your imagination along with those beans.

Bottled Cucumber

Grow your own cucumber garden.

What You'll Need:

Two-liter soda bottle, soil, cucumber seeds, nut pick, water, sunshine

TO ADD AN interesting twist to a cucumber, grow one in a bottle. Take a two-liter plastic soda bottle and poke several ventilation holes in it. When cucumbers start to develop, gently insert them (still attached to their vines) through the bottle's top. Shade the bottle with some cucumber leaves so that the small cukes won't cook from too much heat. Water every few days. You might have to try this with several cucumbers before you get one to full size—but eventually it will work!

Good Old Days

Gardeners are lucky to live in modern times.

What You'll Need:
Sharp rock, digging stick, seeds, clay pots for water

IF WE NEED gardening tools, we just pull out our cash and head for the lawn and garden supply store. But it wasn't always so. Not so long ago, our ancestors had to make their own tools, often relying on sharp sticks and stones to help break up the soil. So the next time you plant a garden, step back in time a few hundred years. Plant one section the old-fashioned way—with rocks and sticks for gardening tools and seeds your ancient ancestors might have had. Take it a step further and carry water in clay pots to give your growing plants a drink. You'll get a whole new appreciation for how easy this tough job has become.

My Family Flag

Your family colors—or America's—in bloom.

What You'll Need:
Paper, pencils or pens, garden spot, gardening tools, colorful bedding plants (petunias work well)

DOES YOUR FAMILY have its own crest? If not, maybe it's time you made one! Design a family symbol or flag on paper. Make it simple but unique to your "clan." Then plant colorful bedding plants with that design in a big, easy-to-see flower bed. If you can't think of a family flag, plant a design like the good old Stars and Stripes of the American flag and watch your neighbors grin.

Dig it Up

Use these tips before you plant to pick the perfect piece of soil.

What You'll Need:
Soil checklist
(at right)

CHOOSE A PLACE that gets six or more hours of direct sunshine each day. Your garden needs that life-giving light. Make sure your plot of ground is near a water source, a hose, or an irrigation spout. Be sure your land is level so water won't run off (taking your seeds and topsoil with it). Make sure the soil is alive—search for organisms like worms and organic matter like sticks and leaf bits to help feed your crops. With these tips in mind, you're sure to be a real green thumb.

1. Make sure your garden plot is weed-free.

2. Remove large rocks from your soil before you plant.

3. Add compost or manure to your soil for extra nutrients.

4. Are earthworms a part of your garden? If not, add some.

Respiring Plants

How do plants take in oxygen?

What You'll Need:
Leafy plant,
petroleum jelly,
paper and pen

EVEN THOUGH plants don't have nostrils or mouths like people do, they still need to take in air. There's a way to find out how plants breathe. Just take a small plant that has plenty of leaves and place it on an outdoor windowsill. Cover the tops (not the bottoms) of five of the plant's leaves with a thick coating of petroleum jelly. Then, cover the bottom sides only of five *other* leaves with another thick layer of jelly. Make a chart and keep track of how each leaf looks every day. Watch your plant for a week, and see if you can figure out which side of the leaf needs to be uncoated in order to bring in fresh air.

Grass Flowers

Do grasses have flowers? Use your observation skills to learn.

What You'll Need:
Grassy meadow that you can visit often, magnifying glass

WHAT IS A FLOWER? The reproductive part of a flowering plant. A flower may have anthers that make pollen, an ovary that makes seeds, or both. Plants pollinated by insects have bright petals, but plants pollinated by wind don't need to "advertise."

Visit a grassy meadow in early spring, just when the grasses form their seed heads. Observe the heads with your magnifying glass. Green or papery structures called "bracts" hold the seed. Return to the meadow until you see small dangling structures sticking out between the bracts. Some are anthers, which make pollen. They hang outside of the bracts so that when they ripen and split open, pollen scatters to the wind.

Sun-Dried Fruit

Use the power of the sun to make tasty fruit snacks.

What You'll Need:
Fruit (apples, plums, peaches, apricots, pears), peeler (optional), safe knife, lemon juice (optional), one-inch-deep baking dishes, cheesecloth, tape

WATCH THE WEATHER reports and make sure that sun is predicted for several days, because it may take that long to dry your fruit. Wash the fruit and peel it if you like. Remove seeds or cores and slice the fruit one-quarter of an inch thick. If you want, dip the fruit in lemon juice to keep it from turning quite so brown. Spread the fruit slices in baking dishes. Cover the dishes with a layer of cheesecloth to keep the insects off. Tape the edges of the cheesecloth into place. Check the fruit each night.

Drying Your Herbs

Hang your favorite herbs out to dry.

What You'll Need:
Dark, dry place, safe plant shears, string, clothespins, airtight spice containers, labels

Once you grow your herbs, transplant them to an outside garden, and watch them thrive, it's time for the harvest. The best time to harvest most herbs is just as they begin to bloom. Once you pick them, run a string across a dry, dark place just outside your back door or a window. Add a dozen or more clothespins across that line of string. Now hang your favorite herbs roots up, top-leaf-down on that string. As the herbs dry and crumble, take them down and store them in labeled, airtight containers until you're ready to use them for cooking!

Garden Nite-Nite

Eating isn't the last step when it comes to your garden.

What You'll Need:
Garden clippers, rake

Even if your garden has been a huge success—you've grown and eaten strawberries, green beans, corn, or watermelons—your work as a farmer isn't finished. If you love the land, the onset of winter means payback time. Before the snow and chill officially arrive, put your garden to bed. Gently clip down what's left of your plants and rake them back into your garden plot. That will feed the soil during the long, winter months and help make it full of nutrients come next year. If you take care of your garden in the winter, it will take care of you next spring.

Seed Pot

Protecting yesterday's seeds for tomorrow's harvest.

What You'll Need:
Modeling clay,
oven,
aluminum foil,
tempera paint,
seeds

Ancient tribes kept their precious seeds in clay pots for safekeeping between planting seasons. You can make a seed pot of your own. Buy some inexpensive modeling clay at your local craft store. (Be sure it's the kind of clay that bakes to a permanent finish in your oven.) Now mold a clay pot with a fairly broad opening, or "mouth." Roll a clay ball just big enough to fit in that clay opening without slipping inside the pot.

With help, bake both pieces in your oven on a cookie sheet lined with aluminum foil at the temperature and time length mentioned on the clay packaging. Once the pot cools, paint them on the outside with tempera paint. Then keep your leftover and collected seeds safe and dry until it's time to plant again. You'll be following in some proud and ancient footsteps when you do.

Save a Seed

Recycle seeds nature's way.

What You'll Need:
Summer plants as
they begin to seed,
jar, coffee can, or
seed pot with lid

Long before there were seed companies, farmers collected the seeds from one season's plants and put them away for the next year's planting. You can do the same thing. When your plants, or the plants of a neighbor, stop growing and go dormant, gather up the seeds for planting next spring. It's the best way to recycle—nature-style!

Night and Day Scent Tower

Grow vines with scented flowers that you can enjoy day and night!

What You'll Need:

Moonflower seeds, sandpaper, cup, warm water, sweet pea seeds, large pot (12 inches or wider) with saucer, potting soil, three bamboo poles about six feet long, string, safe scissors

WAIT UNTIL SPRING warms up before planting these flowers. Notice that moonflower seeds are as hard as rocks. Take six seeds and place them between two sheets of sandpaper. Rub the sheets together for about a minute. Then put the seeds in warm water to soak overnight. The sandpaper roughs up the seed coat, which can then soak up water to help the seeds germinate.

Now soak six sweet pea seeds in warm water overnight (they don't need sanding). While the seeds soak, fill the pot with soil to within about one inch of the rim. Water the soil well. Take three bamboo poles and tie them together at one end. Spread the other ends and stick them in the pot to form a tripod for your plants to climb. After your seeds have soaked, plant them an inch or two apart around the edge of the pot. Set the pot in a warm, sunny place. Keep the soil moist, but not soggy.

When the vines are tall, they will flower. Sweet peas, which bloom in the day, have a sweet, spicy scent. Moonflowers bloom at night. Their rich perfume attracts big luna moths.

A Real Perennial

The oldest known garden plant is the plant of St. Gall monastery, dated A.D. 820. The monks of that time grew fruit trees, vegetables, herbs, lilies, and roses—plants that we still grow today!

Garden Bird Bath

Beautiful—and useful, too.

What You'll Need:
Old pie pans, ceramic bowls, or anything you can fill with a shallow pool of water

GARDENS ARE beautiful in their own right—green and growing and full of wonder. But a garden alive with birds is special. If you scatter bird baths across your garden, you'll have a graceful show that controls insect infestation. Find old pie tins, ceramic bowls, or other containers that will hold shallow pools of water throughout your garden. Keep them filled with fresh, clean water (refill the pools when you water your plants). But remember, birds like to eat berries. So if you invite them, they may nibble some of the goods you wanted to eat yourself.

What Lives in a Tree?

Discover a tree's smallest inhabitants.

What You'll Need:
A tree with an easy-to-reach branch, white bed sheet, a partner, magnifying glass

HAVE A PARTNER help you stretch a white sheet under a tree branch. (The closer you hold the sheet to the branch, the better.) Shake the branch hard for about a minute, then lay the sheet on the ground and observe with a magnifying glass. What tiny animals do you see? Look for spiders, adult insects, and caterpillars. Now try the same activity with a different tree. Do you find the same animals in a pine that you do in an oak? Record your findings and compare. Try sampling the same tree several times in a year. Do you see different insects at different times?

Taste Test Garden

How long is a matter of taste!

What You'll Need:
Carrot or radish patch,
pad of paper,
pencil

WHEN IS THE best time to harvest your garden crops? Read your seed envelope instructions, then try this experiment. Beginning about one week before your carrots or radishes are supposed to be ripe, pull a single sample and take a healthy bite (make sure you clean the dirt off and rinse the sample first). How does it taste seven days early? Write it down. How about six days early? Five days early? And so on. When you plant your garden the next year, you'll know *exactly* how long it takes to grow the garden that you think tastes just right.

Something Nutty

Go nuts! Grow nuts!

What You'll Need:
Peanut seeds or starts

WHY GROW CARROTS when you can go completely nuts? Try your hand at growing delicious peanuts. You can buy seeds from a gardening store, or even raw peanuts from the grocery store—the same nuts you like to munch on will grow into new plants! Remove the shells and plant the seeds about three-quarters of an inch deep in sandy soil, about a foot apart, in the spring. Mound the soil around the plants after they flower to help with pollination. In about four months, your peanuts will mature—you'll know it's time when the leaves start to turn yellow. Remember, your harvest will be underground. Peanuts are actually roots!

Toadville

You know that toads don't REALLY give us warts. Did you know they eat lots of insect pests, too?

What You'll Need:
Broken ceramic flower pot or bowl, mosses and soft leaves, plenty of moisture

WHY NOT INVITE those little croakers to move in by creating toad habitats just for their amphibious ways? Use a broken pot or bowl turned with the curved side up as a toad shelter. Line the ground beneath the pot with moist mosses and leaves. Make sure you put the pots near an area sure to be watered. Then wait for the toads to arrive. They'll eat lots of bugs and give you plenty to look at.

Grass Prints

Grass seed heads make beautiful lacy prints.

What You'll Need:
Grasses of various kinds (include seed heads), paper, wax paper, water-based paints, paintbrush, cloth (optional)

LAY YOUR GRASSES OUT on a table and choose those you like the best. Arrange the grasses you like on paper. Try making interesting contrasts between lacy seed heads and thick grass blades. To make your prints, lay the grass on wax paper. Load a brush with paint and dab the paint on the grass until it is thinly but fully coated on one side.

Lift the painted grass from the wax paper and lay it, paint side down, on the paper you want to print. Lay another sheet of wax paper on top and press gently so that the grass makes good contact with the paper. Remove the wax paper and grass. Watercolor paint works on white paper, while tempera looks nice on colored paper. Use fabric paint on cloth to make beautiful grass-printed T-shirts and bandannas!

Living Bouquets

If you have no room for flower beds, use a pot or window box!

What You'll Need:
Flowerpots (at least
12 inches across)
with saucers,
purchased plants,
potting soil,
plant fertilizer

PLANTING LIVING bouquets outdoors in big pots is especially fun if you pick out your own plants! Go to a garden center, choose some annuals (plants that die at the end of the growing season), then see what kinds of plants look nice together. Go for leaf combinations, too, such as dark green and silvery, fuzzy leaves.

When you get home, pour some soil into large pots, set the plants gently in them, and fill in soil in around them. Water until the liquid runs out the pots and into the saucers. Set the pots in a sunny place. Water daily (twice a day in hot weather) and pick off dry or dying leaves. Feed the plants with a good plant fertilizer, following instructions on the label.

Leaf Litter

Discover organisms that turn fallen leaves into good soil.

What You'll Need:
Garden gloves,
magnifying glass

FIND A PLACE in the woods where leaves pile up. Look away from trampled paths or under big shrubs. Move aside the surface layer of leaves. Underneath, you'll find crumbled leaves. Under *that,* the remains of the leaves look like soil. How do leaves become soil? Bacteria and fungi rot leaves, but they also get help from larger organisms.

Use your magnifying glass to look at each layer of litter. What do you see? In the upper layers, you may find beetles eating dead leaves. In moist areas, millipedes break leaves into small pieces that bacteria and fungi work on. In deep layers, spiders, centipedes, and springtails eat bits of leaves crumbled from weathering or broken up by larger bugs. In low layers near the soil, earthworms eat soil and decayed leaves.

Water Garden

A water garden—a small pond alive with plants and growing things—is not as hard to build as you might think.

What You'll Need:
Large tub or pot,
plants,
water,
goldfish,
snails,
de-icer (optional)

Pick any LARGE tub or pot that will securely hold fresh water. Add common oxygenating plants like anacharis, Parrot's feather, and moneywort. Then add edge/bog plants like pickerel rush, zebra rush, and cattails. Top it all off with delicate floating water lilies, then add your goldfish and snails. Make sure your water garden has at least six hours of sunlight a day and be careful not to use pesticides; they could kill your fish in a matter of minutes. If you live in a town with a very cold winter, use a fish-safe de-icer on your pond and the fish should survive. Check with your local garden center to be sure.

Pineapple Party

Grow your own tangy beauties from just a leaf.

What You'll Need:
Pineapple,
shallow pan,
water, pot, soil

Believe it or not, you can use the leafy end of a store-bought pineapple to grow a great plant. In fact, it may even triple its size by the time 12 months have passed. Just pick a pineapple with a good, leafy top. Cut that top off, leaving about an inch of fruit attached. Set the pineapple top in a shallow pan, like an old layer cake pan, filled with water. Once it begins to root, plant it in rich soil and keep the dirt moist (but not too wet). To protect the tropical wonder from extreme cold, bring it inside when the weather drops below 45 degrees.

Seed Collection

Collect seeds and discover nature's tiny treasures!

What You'll Need:

Envelopes or clear film canisters, seeds, newspaper, cardboard (optional), glue (optional), paper (optional), pen (optional)

BEFORE YOU BEGIN, decide how you want to organize your collection. Clear plastic film canisters are useful for storing seeds; they are waterproof and you can see the seeds. Ask for them at any store that develops film. You can also store seeds in paper envelopes, which can be kept in a shoebox.

Collect seeds in late summer and fall. Watch for wild fruits to ripen. Remove the seeds from the fruits and let them dry on newspaper before storing them. Watch for maple seeds to drop. Oaks will drop acorns in the fall. These are seeds, too. Let pine cones dry indoors, then pull out the scales and look for seeds. As flowers finish blooming, leave some on the plant so you can collect the seeds they make. To collect weed seeds, wear socks over your shoes and walk through weeds or a meadow. Look at the seeds stuck to your socks!

Make sure the seeds are dry before you store them, or they will mold. Put each kind of seed in a different container. If you want to make a seed display, glue different kinds of seeds to cardboard and make a paper label for each.

Ancient Pro-Seed-ure

Native Americans who farmed along the rivers of the Great Plains were very familiar with gathering and re-planting seeds. They grew corn, beans, and sunflowers, and even enjoyed sunflower seed snacks as we do today.

Lawn Census

How do lawn plants and animals adapt in order to survive?

What You'll Need:
Lawn,
magnifying glass
(optional),
notebook,
pencil

WHEN YOUR LAWN is ready to be mowed, investigate what lives there. Find out what kind of grass should grow there. Look for grass of a different color or with larger or smaller blades. Find different kinds of weeds. You may not have names for all the plants, but you can describe and draw them in your notebook.

Then get down on your hands and knees and look for animal life. Use your magnifying glass to discover beetles, spiders, worms, grubs, and other lawn animals. Write down what you see.

The morning after the lawn is mowed, do a second survey. Are the same weeds still alive? Is it the way they grow that helps them survive? Some weeds creep between grass blades, while some form flat, saucer-like rosettes of leaves that smother the grass and stay away from mower blades. Hunt for lawn animals again. How do *they* avoid the mower?

Plant Buddies

Some plants rely on others to help them grow.

What You'll Need:
Mossy tree,
your own powers
of observation

WHEN YOU'RE IN a forest, look for plants that grow on trees. Scientists call these plants epiphytes. Their relationship is symbiotic, a scientific word that means "living together." Moss is an epiphyte. Look closely at moss growing on a tree. Moss, a simple plant, does not have true roots, but tiny root-like structures help the plant cling to the side of the tree. Bits of dead bark collect and rot, providing nutrients for the moss. Look for other epiphytes. In some areas, licorice fern grows on oak tree limbs. Mistletoe, another epiphyte, is a parasite. Its roots bore into oaks and spruces and draw out moisture and sap.

Hummingbird Honey

Attract these little wonders to your garden.

What You'll Need:
Plants,
water,
shade and sun

Dɪᴅ you ᴋɴow that hummingbirds have no sense of smell? It's true. They depend on sight, not scent, to find the flowers from which they love to drink. But if you plant a garden alive with the plants they crave, they will make your yard a hummingbird haven.

Which plants you use depends on where you live. In the Southwest, you might plant red sages or honeysuckle; in the Pacific Northwest, currants or Indian paintbrushes; in the Southeast, trumpet creepers or mimosas; and in the Midwest and Northeast, bee balms and red buckeyes.

Ask your local nursery manager for other plant suggestions. And remember, red is a hummingbird favorite. Be sure your garden has shade as well as sunshine, and always water with a fine mist. Hummingbirds love to bathe in misty water clouds.

Wagon Wonders

Planting smaller gardens in creative places can be fun!

What You'll Need:
Red wagon,
soil,
bedding plants

Pʟᴀɴᴛ ᴀ ʀᴇᴅ, white, and blue garden in your favorite little red wagon and you'll not only have a fun flowerbed, but you will also have a fourth of July float for a neighborhood parade. Use simple bedding plants like petunias in bedding soil. Keep them watered, but not too wet. Before you know it, you'll have a beautiful garden on wheels.

Tree Story Book

Make your own books to help you learn about trees.

What You'll Need:
White paper,
9" x 12" colored
construction paper,
stapler, pencil or
pen, glue, tree
identification book,
crayons

To MAKE A tree book, fold two sheets of white paper in half. Fold the construction paper in half and insert the white paper. Staple together along the spine. Make one book for each kind of tree you're interested in. Take a photo of the tree (or draw it) and glue the picture to the cover of the book. Learn the tree's name from an adult or at the library.

Hold the first page of the book against the tree's bark. Rub a crayon over the page to make a pattern. Pick a leaf, flatten it, and glue it into your book. If your tree sheds flowers, pick and press one. If your tree loses branches, find a small winter twig. Glue it on the third page. Then use pages four and five to describe what is living in the tree.

A Tree Speaks

Trees can tell us their stories if we learn to "read" their marks.

What You'll Need:
Recently cut tree
stump,
coarse sandpaper,
magnifying glass

IF A TREE HAS been recently cut in your neighborhood, ask to see the stump. If you have trouble seeing the rings on the stump, sand the surface with coarse sandpaper. Count the rings to see how old the tree is. Notice that light and dark rings alternate. The wider, lighter-colored rings are springwood, laid down when the tree grew rapidly in early spring. Narrower, darker-colored rings are summerwood.

Narrow rings on one side of the tree mean that the tree was stressed on that side. Perhaps it was shaded by another tree, or building construction damaged the roots. Narrow rings all around show that the tree was stressed for several years. There may have been a drought; maybe insects ate too many of its leaves.

Leaf Scents

Can you tell your trees by scent alone?

What You'll Need:
Leaves of various trees

IF YOU'VE EVER smelled herbs, either fresh on the vine or in kitchen jars, you know that leaves can have powerful scents. Some we like very much and use for cooking or perfumes. Others we don't like at all. All leaves have distinctive scents, though most aren't as strong as herbs. Find out for yourself what tree leaves smell like.

Start with trees or shrubs in your own yard. Pick a leaf from a tree and crush it in your hand. Hold it to your nose and sniff. What does it smell like? Can you describe the scent? Some leaves smell musty. Conifers have a strong pine-oil odor. Other leaves may smell fresh or sharp. Try this with as many kinds of trees and shrubs as you can find. Then test yourself. Close your eyes and have someone crush a leaf for you to smell, or make a pile of different leaves and draw from it with your eyes closed. Can you identify trees and shrubs by their scents?

Strawbarrel

Berry much fun in a little bitty space.

What You'll Need:
Large planting pot, potting soil, strawberry starts, water

EVEN IF you don't have room for a garden, you probably have room for a strawbarrel. Fill a large half-barrel or outdoor planter with good, rich garden soil or potting soil. Then plant six strawberry starts (which you can buy at any garden store) in the soil. Make certain to water your berry plants every day, keeping the soil damp but not soaking wet. Also make sure your berries get at least six hours of sunlight a day. Before you know it, you'll be gobbling strawberries you grew yourself—even if you live downtown!

Seed Bank

Plants save for a rainy day by putting their seeds in seed banks!

What You'll Need:
Clean soil,
trowel,
aluminum baking
pan, water,
plastic wrap

SEEDS THAT fall to the ground don't grow right away. They wait until conditions are right. To grow plants from a seed bank yourself, collect soil from any natural area (such as a dark forest or under a shrub) that hasn't had herbicides or pesticides applied to it. Scrape away any decaying plant material and dig enough soil to fill your pan one-half to one inch deep.

Water the soil so that it is moist but not soggy. Cover the pan with plastic wrap to keep it moist and warm. Set in a warm place and wait. After about a week, young plants will be growing. Where do they come from? They sprouted from seeds already in the soil. This is what we call a seed bank. Try this with soil from various places. How is the seed bank in a forest different from the seed bank in a meadow? Try garden soil too.

Mini-Garden

Victorian kids made "fairy gardens." Create your own version!

What You'll Need:
Shady 3' x 3' garden
spot (get permission),
rocks, sticks, and
moss, shade-loving
plants, trowel,
toy animals or dolls

IN THE SHELTER of a large, shady shrub, you can design a miniature world. Use dolls and toy animals as inhabitants, if you like, or pretend (as Victorian children did) that the "little people" visit your garden when you're not looking. First, decide where the edges of your garden will be. Mark the edges with a tiny wall made of rocks or sticks. Use stones to make paths. Build miniature houses by stacking sticks log-cabin style. Cover the houses with moss. Fill the rest of the space with shade-loving plants, such as annuals like impatiens, coleus, polka-dot plants, and violas, or perennials like dwarf ferns, dwarf hostas, and violets.

Useful Cattails

Native Americans used cattails in many ways. So can you!

What You'll Need:
A place to gather fresh cattails, a paper bag, large piece of corrugated cardboard, thumbtacks, safe scissors, glue

CATTAILS PROVIDED food and fibers for Native Americans. If cattails grow abundantly near *your* home, pull one up. The crispy rootstalk and the base of the leaves are edible, but only if grown in unpolluted water. Some plants with poisonous roots grow in wet areas. NEVER eat things you don't recognize.

Pollen from cattail heads is edible. Shake the yellow heads into a paper bag. Cattail pollen, rich in protein, can mix with flour and go into bread, biscuits, and pancakes.

You can even use the leaves to make placemats! Lay some long leaves side by side on a large sheet of cardboard. Thumbtack one end of each leaf to the cardboard to hold it in place. Weave more leaves in and out. Trim the leaves. When you finish weaving, trim the ends with scissors and let the mat dry. Dab glue under each cut end. This will hold the mat together.

Sunny Flower Garden

Plants from the nursery make a colorful splash in your yard.

What You'll Need:
4' x 3' garden patch (get permission), shovel, bagged compost, bagged mulch (optional), plants, trowel, hose, small sprinkler

CHOOSE A GARDEN spot that gets six or more hours of sun a day. Pull weeds and dig up soil until it crumbles. Spread a one-inch layer of bagged compost over the soil and mix it in. Then buy plants at a garden center. Buy small, healthy annuals that aren't flowering.

Set your plants on the bed and arrange them. Give the young plants plenty of room. With your trowel, dig a hole for each plant. Turn the pot over and tap the plant into your hand. Loosen the root ball with your fingers, and set the roots into the soil. Water your plants with a sprinkler every few days. Pick your flowers often to keep the plants blooming.

Flower Scents

All flowers have a scent, though it may be hard to notice.

What You'll Need:
Flowers of various kinds

SCENT IS ONE way to attract insects, which have keen senses of smell. Strongly scented flowers like lavender, roses, and lilies need powerful smells to attract insects. Flowers pollinated by hummingbirds don't have scents—birds don't have a good sense of smell. But do these flowers have *any* odor?

Go through the yard and collect several types of open flowers. (Get permission first.) Do they have scents? Some will have a strong, obvious odor, but others will have little or no odor. Take the flowers that don't have much smell and crush them in your hand. All flowers have some sort of scent. Next, close your eyes and have a friend hold crushed flowers under your nose. Can you identify flowers by smell alone?

Bean Teepee

Make a cool, leafy hiding place in the summer!

What You'll Need:
4' x 4' garden patch, eight-12 bamboo stakes at least six feet long, string, safe scissors, pole bean seeds (such as scarlet runner bean or blue lake)

IN LATE SPRING, when the weather warms up, pick a spot in the garden about four feet on each side. Make sure the ground is ready to plant. (See "Sunny Flower Garden" on page 29 if you're starting with uncultivated soil.) Tie your stakes together at the top and set them upright in the middle of the patch. Spread the bottom ends out to make a circle. Leave an opening between two stakes wide enough for a "door."

Soak your bean seeds overnight, then plant four or five an inch deep at the bottom of each pole. Keep the seeds watered while they sprout. They should find the stakes themselves and climb upwards. By midsummer, your bean teepee should be ready. Spread a tarp inside and call your friends!

Flying Seeds

Discover how the wind can send some seeds flying.

What You'll Need:
Wind-dispersed seeds (maple, elm, dandelion, thistle), partner, home with a second-story window, sticks (optional)

In THE FALL, collect wind-blown seeds. Look for seeds with wings, such as maple and elm, or with downy parachutes, like the dandelion or thistle. These seeds are built so that the wind will scatter them far from their parent plant. Have your partner stand carefully near an open window on the second floor of a home and toss a handful of winged seeds toward the ground.

Watch them to see how far they sail. If possible, mark the furthest seed with a tall stick. Note also how the seeds land. Do they fall flat, or do they spin so fast that they drill themselves into the ground? Now have your partner drop dandelion or thistle seeds. (Make sure they are separated from one another first.) Do they drop to the ground, or do they float for miles? Can you mark the farthest one? Try activity on a breezy day and a still day to compare how far the seeds spread.

Kinda Corny

Plant for a colorful harvest!

What You'll Need:
Indian corn seeds, small, sunny square of ground

Do you LOVE the way that colorful brown, yellow, and orange Indian corn brightens up the autumn? You can plant your own series of stalks long before the summer turns to fall. Head for your favorite general or gardening store in March, April, or May. Gather up seed packets of colorful corn varieties. Plant them as instructed on the packages. By the time fall comes around, you'll have grown your own rainbow of maize to harvest and enjoy.

Weather Wonders

How's the weather today? What will it be like tomorrow? Ever since ancient times people have asked the same questions. While modern weather instruments can give us better and better long-range forecasts, the weather wisdom of our ancestors is still useful today. Learn to watch for weather signs, as people did long ago, and make some modern weather instruments of your own. Try making your own weather predictions based on what you've learned and see how often your predictions come true. Maybe you'll develop sympathy for the weather forecasters on television!

 ## Rainy-Day Pictures

Create your own masterpiece—with a little help from the rain!

What You'll Need:
Paper,
water-soluble
paint or markers

You've probably used lots of things to create pieces of art, like paint, markers, tissue paper, string, and even rocks. But have you ever used the rain to make a piece of artwork? This idea may sound all wet, but give it a try!

Use your paint or markers to draw shapes and lines on a piece of paper. Then bring on the rain! Place your piece of paper in the rain for about 20 seconds. When you take your "canvas" out of the rain, dry it out, and then check out your creation. Thanks to the rain, your shapes and lines will have turned into something else entirely!

What's the Weather Like?

You don't need a crystal ball to predict when it's going to rain. All it takes is a little practice!

What You'll Need:
Radio,
notepad,
pen or pencil

PREDICTING THE WEATHER isn't a cinch, but you can look for hints about whether it's about to rain. First, listen to the weather report on the radio. If rain is on the way, grab a notepad and head out. There are plenty of signs in nature to alert you if umbrella weather is coming. For instance, some flowers—like tulips and dandelions—close up when rain is heading in. Clover folds its leaves. Some trees know it's going to rain, so they turn their leaves over to keep their tops dry. Many spiders take down their webs before a heavy rainstorm. Cows gather together and lie down in a field before the rain hits, and dogs often smell the air before a rainfall.

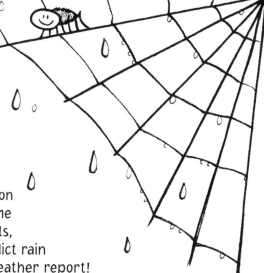

You'll also notice that noises are a lot clearer and smells are much stronger just before it rains. When you're outside, keep an eye, ear, or nose out to see if any of these things happen around your home. Write them on your notepad. If you do the same thing before a few more rainfalls, you'll see how easy it is to predict rain without even listening to the weather report!

Weather journal

Document your weather trends.

What You'll Need:
Notebook,
pencil or pen

KEEPING A WEATHER journal can teach you about weather patterns and help you forecast the weather conditions to come. Just get an ordinary spiral notebook at your grocery or department store. Check the weather outside, watch the forecast on television, and make a few notes each day. Now go outside, watch the weather, and add your own personal notes to those mentioned on TV. See if you can guess what the weather will be like the next day and write down your prediction. (Be sure to mention in the next day's entry if your prediction was right!) Before you know it, you'll begin to recognize weather trends. You'll be a junior weather forecaster, even if you never get to make your predictions on TV.

Stay Cool, Stay Warm

The way you dress can affect your personal environment.

What You'll Need:
Two identical
drinking glasses,
one sheet of
black paper,
one sheet of
white paper, tape,
water, thermometer

WHETHER THE WEATHER is hot or cold, the colors you wear can affect your body temperature. Want to test the theory? Take two identical drinking glasses. Wrap one in black paper and tape it securely. Wrap the other in white paper and tape it in place. Now fill both glasses with lukewarm water and put them on a porch or picnic table. Allow the glasses to stand undisturbed in direct sunlight for about an hour. Now use a thermometer to measure the temperature of the water inside each glass. Then decide which color of clothes will help you stay warm or cool. Odds are that your choice will be crystal clear.

Get Wet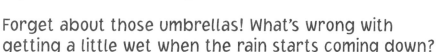

Forget about those umbrellas! What's wrong with getting a little wet when the rain starts coming down?

What You'll Need:
Raincoat,
rain hat,
waterproof boots

Don't STAY COOPED UP in the house when there's a downpour. Toss on a raincoat and hat and a pair of waterproof boots and head outside! You'll be surprised how different the world is while the rain is coming down.

Once you're outside splashing through the rain, take a big whiff of the air. Do you notice a difference in the smell of rainy-day air? Look around and see if you can spot any animals or insects that you don't normally see when the sun's out.

Watch your step. Chances are you'll see plenty of earthworms wiggling about in the rain.

Some trees have leaves that are made so that the rain glides off them. What other things do you see around your house that look different in the rain than they do when the sun is out?

The Sky Is Falling!

Raindrops aren't all that fall from the sky during a storm. In 1997, live toads rained down on the Mexican town of Villa Angel Flores. Experts think the toads may have been swept up into a tornado and tossed to earth when the winds died down.

Let it Rain

Here's your chance to be a rainy-day detective. Find out what crawls around in your backyard when it rains.

What You'll Need:
Shovel,
glass jar,
piece of cheese,
four small rocks,
piece of wood,
piece of glass or
clear plastic

HERE'S YOUR MISSION... should you choose to accept it! Before it begins to rain, dig a hole in a garden bed and bury a glass jar up to its neck. Make sure the opening of the jar is not covered with dirt. Now place your "bait" (the cheese) in it. Find four small rocks and place them on the dirt around the jar.

Then put a small piece of wood on top of the rocks to keep the rain out of the jar. But be sure there's enough room between the wood and the jar so that the insects and other small creatures can crawl between them. Now your "trap" is set.

Once the rain has stopped, look in the jar to see what creatures went for the cheese. If you "caught" a slug, place it on another piece of glass or a chunk of clear plastic. That way, you can see its underside and watch how it moves. After you've taken a look at all the creatures, let them go on their way. Mission accomplished!

Wet Scent
Have you ever noticed how great the air smells after a rainfall? Well, that's because the rain has cleaned it up! When it rains, raindrops wash away all the dust and dirt that are in the air.

Bottled Cloud

Make a little weather of your own.

What You'll Need:
Candle,
match,
clear glass two-liter
bottle

CLOUDS FORM when warm, particle-rich air meets cool, moist air. This fun activity can help you understand just how it works. On a cool day with little or no wind, head for your backyard and find a table. Ask your parents to help you light a candle. With help, turn your two-liter glass bottle upside down and hold the candle inside the mouth of the jar for about ten seconds. (Don't use a plastic jar. The mouth of a plastic jug could melt.) Once the bottle's mouth has cooled a little, form a seal around the bottle with your mouth and blow. Once you pull your mouth away, you should see a cloud form inside the bottle—just like in the skies above your home.

Tornado, Hold the Mayo

Twirling currents trapped inside a jar.

What You'll Need:
Clear mayonnaise
jar,
water,
food coloring,
liquid dish soap,
vinegar

DO TORNADOES make you dizzy? Do their spinning, twirling winds make you wonder how they work? Well, shake up a tornado of your own with this wild activity and study its spiraling vortex of currents without fear. Fill an ordinary glass mayonnaise jar about two-thirds of the way with water. Add a few drops of food coloring (any color) to the water. Then, add a teaspoon of liquid dish-washing soap and a teaspoon of vinegar. Screw the lid on good and tight to prevent leaks and extreme messes. Give the jar a good, hard shake, then give it a twist to set the liquid inside spinning. What you'll see is a tiny bottled cortex that looks just like a miniature tornado. You'll soon understand how the real thing actually works.

Fun in the Sun

What time is it? Time to make a sundial. Once you build your own sundial, you may never use a watch again!

What You'll Need:
Medium-sized stick,
marker,
watch,
several small
wooden stakes

SUNDIALS HAVE been used for centuries to help tell the time. Now, *you* can learn the secret. Start your sundial bright and early on a day that will be quite sunny. First, place the stick in the ground. (Make sure it's in an area that gets a lot of sun.) Then, place a small stake at the tip of the shadow cast by the stick and write the time on the side. As the sun moves through the sky, the stick's shadow will move. Keep an eye on your watch.

When an hour has passed, place another wooden stake at the tip of the new shadow cast by the stick. Write the time on the side of this stake. Continue to mark the shadows throughout the afternoon and be sure to write the correct time on each stake. When you finish, you'll have a sundial! To find out what time it is, follow the shadow cast by the stick. It'll point to a stake, and you can see the time on the side of the stake!

Weather Bugs Bugs

Does weather slow down your favorite pest?

What You'll Need:
Clean, clear jar with a lid full of air holes, pancake syrup, one captured fly, refrigerator

SUMMER IS DEFINITELY the season of the buzzing, bothersome fly. Hordes of them seem to invade your house and your yard as soon as the weather turns warm. But why do they seem to vanish when the cool, short days return? Cold weather bugs some bugs. This activity will show you how much.

Capture an ordinary housefly in a clear plastic or glass jar (use a bit of pancake syrup to lure your fly into the jar). Be sure the jar has air holes so your experiment subject won't suffer as you hold it captive. See how fast and active the fly is even while inside the jar? Now, place the jar inside your fridge for half an hour.

Retrieve the jar and watch the fly now. Has the temporary chill slowed it down? Release the fly outside once your experiment is complete.

What a Blowhard!

From a breeze to a brawl, you'll know it all.

What You'll Need:
String, hole puncher, safe scissors, crepe paper, newspaper, light cloth, heavy cloth

HOW HARD IS the wind blowing? Find out by making your own simple gauge. Using string, attach four strips cut to equal sizes—one each of crepe paper, newspaper, light cloth, and heavy cloth—to a branch or rain gutter. When the wind blows softly, the crepe paper will react. When it blows a little harder, the newspaper will flutter. As the wind increases in strength, the light cloth will wave. When the heavy cloth flaps, you will know the wind is blowing *hard*.

Blue Skies

How waves of light color your world.

What You'll Need:
Flashlight,
table,
flour

WHY IS THE SKY blue? When the white light of the sun filters through our atmosphere, it scatters into every color of the rainbow and every possible wavelength. Our atmosphere makes it blue. This simple experiment will give you an idea of how that scattering works and why weather patterns can cause a colorful shift.

Turn a flashlight on outside at night. Set the flashlight on a table so its beam shines in midair in front of you. Now sprinkle flour in front of the beam. You should see dozens of white flashes as each piece of flour or dust reflects light waves and sends the color signal straight to your eyes. That's how our atmosphere sends flashes of color to *your* eyes to make the sky seem so blue.

Ballooning Temperature

Give new meaning to the "big bang" theory.

What You'll Need:
Helium balloons,
hot day

CERTAIN GASES expand when exposed to heat. This experiment with helium balloons and hot summer days will show you how—and how much. Fill four balloons with helium at your local party or craft store. Ask the clerk to fill one half-full, one three-quarters-full, one just right, and one a little too full. Be sure your car is running and has the air conditioning on, and that the car is waiting at the entrance of the store when you come out. Once you get home, rush the balloons inside the cool house. One by one, take the balloons outside, starting with the half-full balloon, and watch what happens. You'll see just how helium expands with heat and what that expansion does to the latex in balloons.

Wind Wondering

Any way the wind blows.

What You'll Need:
Crepe paper
streamers,
tape or stapler,
notebook paper,
pen or pencil

WHICH WAY DOES the wind blow? And how does that affect your environment? This colorful experiment will help you find out. Carefully staple or tape six crepe paper streamers, each about two feet long, to a tree branch or clothesline. Anytime you see the paper flutter in the wind, take a few notes. Which way is the wind coming from? How long do the papers stay in motion? Write your notes on a piece of paper for at least one week. At the end of the week, check to see if there are any regular patterns. Does the wind seem to blow mostly from the east? Check the trees and plants growing in your yard. Do they tilt ever so slightly to the east? Could the wind have something to do with the leaning? Who knows for sure? That's what science is all about—asking good questions and doing your best to find answers.

Listen to Lightning

Strike a pose and listen!

What You'll Need:
Thunder

How far away did that last bolt of lightning strike? This easy calculation will make it clear. First, listen for the distant thunder—the sound wave that travels from the center of the super-warmed air surrounding the lightning channel as it expands (like ripples in a pond when you drop a pebble in). But sound travels much more slowly than the flash of electric light—about a million times slower. So when you see the light, start counting. For every five seconds that pass between the site of lightning and the sound of the thunder, the strike is about one mile away. Ten seconds? Two miles away, and so on.

Avalanche!

Simulated disasters help you understand the real thing.

What You'll Need:
Cardboard box (cut in half, corner to corner), mittens, cold water, snow

Ever wondered how an avalanche works? Try this activity on for size. On a cold day, cut a cardboard box in half, corner to corner, creating a cardboard peak that will sit flat on the ground. Wet the box and let it freeze, peak to the sky. Once it's frozen, wet it again to create a second, smoother layer of ice. Now let snow blanket the icy peak. Will the snow slide off that steep sheet of ice? A soft bump will help you find out—and simulate a real avalanche.

Snow Goggle Giggles

Long ago, people used goggles to fight snow blindness.
You can use them for fun.

What You'll Need:

Cardboard or Styrofoam egg carton, safe scissors, string or yarn, feathers, sequins, and other odds and ends for decoration

TRIBES THAT CALLED the frigid arctic regions home had a problem with the brightness of unending snow fields. Too much exposure to the reflection of the sun off the snow could cause blindness, so ancient folks crafted goggles to cut down on the wintery glare. Chances are you don't live in those remote snowy regions, so you can make the goggles just for fun.

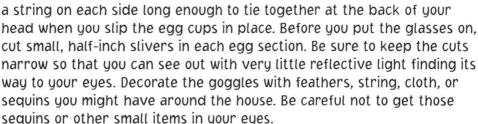

Cut two sections (one for each eye) out of an ordinary egg carton. Tie them together at the nose bridge with soft yarn or string. Now attach a string on each side long enough to tie together at the back of your head when you slip the egg cups in place. Before you put the glasses on, cut small, half-inch slivers in each egg section. Be sure to keep the cuts narrow so that you can see out with very little reflective light finding its way to your eyes. Decorate the goggles with feathers, string, cloth, or sequins you might have around the house. Be careful not to get those sequins or other small items in your eyes.

When It Rains, It Pours

How much water does the average storm let loose?

What You'll Need:
Plastic measuring cup or rain gauge, notebook, pen or pencil

THEY ALWAYS SAY, "When it rains, it pours." But is that really true? Does it really pour, or is the average rainfall in your hometown more like a spurt or a trickle? Find out with this fun experiment.

The next time it looks like rain, place a measuring cup or rain gauge (available at most home and gardening stores) in a clear spot in your yard. Be sure to secure it by anchoring it in the ground or surrounding it with gravel so it doesn't tip over before you gather your information.

Watch the clock and make a note of how many ounces of rain you collect every two hours. Do the same during the next storm—and the next. Now compare your figures to calculate whether it rains when it pours, or just gets things a little damp.

Hail! Hail! The Gang's All Here!

Sometimes the sky rains solid.

What You'll Need:
Large plastic bowls, gravel or sand, aluminum foil, plastic wrap, wax paper, large rubber bands

HOW POWERFUL is your average hailstorm? Try this experiment to find out if the hail in your area even makes a dent. The next time you anticipate a hailstorm, half-fill three large, plastic bowls with sand. Then cover the top of the bowls, one with foil, one with plastic wrap, one with wax paper. Use rubber bands to hold the paper in place. Set the bowls in the open space, where the hail will strike often. Once the storm is over, examine the different bowls. What happened to the foil? The plastic wrap? The wax paper? Explore the impact of hail firsthand.

Gum Wrapper Thermometer

Make a simple thermometer and find out how hot it really is!

What You'll Need:
Foil gum wrapper (foil on one side and paper on the other), safe scissors, spool (or similar item), tape, glue, index cards, pencil or pen, store-bought thermometer

FOIL GUM WRAPPERS are made of two different materials: metal foil and paper. Both react a little differently to heat. The metal foil actually expands a little bit more than the paper as it gets hot. Because the different layers of the wrapper expand and contract at different rates, the wrapper will actually bend as the temperature changes.

Cut a long pointer from a gum wrapper. Tape one end of the pointer to the side of a spool. Glue the spool on its end atop an index card. That's all there is to it! But wait—how do you know how hot or cold it is? If you want actual numbers, you'll have to check a regular thermometer. Once you do that, mark the current temperature on the index card wherever the pointer is pointing to. When the temperature changes, mark the new temperature on your homemade thermometer. You'll find that the gum wrapper thermometer isn't terribly precise; humidity can affect its accuracy. Still, it can tell you whether it is hotter today than yesterday, and maybe that's all the precision you want!

Watch Your Skin!
Did you know that if you're not careful, you can get a sunburn even on a cloudy day? Ultraviolet radiation that comes from the sun can go right through clouds, especially if the cloud layer is thin.

Sun-Baked

What will the sun do to your skin?

What You'll Need:
Soft leather scraps, block of wood, stapler, sunscreen, baby oil, water

EVER WONDERED what too much sun can do to your skin? To get an idea, try this weird and wacky experiment using soft leather scraps. Take four scraps of leather and staple them to a block of wood. Rub a thick layer of sunscreen across the top of one strip, baby oil over another, and water on another. Leave the last one natural.

On a very hot summer day, take the strips of leather outside and let them bake in the sun. The next hot, sunny day, reapply the sunscreen, baby oil, and water and repeat the process. Keep doing this every hot, sunny day. At the end of the summer, closely examine how the strips of leather held up. Now imagine that the leather is your own skin.

Who (or What) Can Resist?

How can you stay dry when it rains?

What You'll Need:
Cotton balls, scraps of five different fabrics, old newspapers, stapler, piece of scrap wood, staple remover

WHICH CLOTHES serve you best when you're caught in a sudden storm? Let a cotton ball be your guide. Take five ordinary cotton balls and five scraps of different fabrics and set them out on a table covered with old newspapers the next time it's ready to rain. Put the cotton balls on a scrap of wood and cover them with squares of cloth.

Be sure to staple the cloth to the wood so the wind doesn't disrupt your experiment. Leave the wood in the rain for about five minutes. Then bring it inside and use a staple remover to peel back the cloth, one cotton ball at a time. Which cotton ball stayed the driest? Which balls are completely soaked? What you find will help you decide what kind of coat to use when it rains.

Animal Instincts

Can the mood of your pet help you predict weather shifts?

What You'll Need:
Pet,
weather forecasts,
notebook,
pencil

Do you HAVE a pet cat, dog, or rabbit? Does the weather affect your animal's moods? Keep track of how pets act on sunny and stormy days. Do they get restless when a rain storm is about to hit? Do they get sleepy when the day is bound to get hot? Do they pace when a hurricane is approaching? Watch closely and keep good notes of how they act before and after the weather changes. Soon, you'll know if your pet suffers from any weather-related moods—and if they can foretell weather patterns or trends.

Can Animals Fly? Yes!

Animals play a large part in the history of air travel. In 1782, two French brothers began test flights with hot-air balloons. They even sent a sheep, a duck, and a rooster up on a flight! The animals went on an eight-minute, two-mile trip before the balloon touched down safely.

Snow Painting

Art on a snowy canvas.

What You'll Need:
Food coloring,
water,
old bowl,
paintbrushes,
old, warm clothing

THE NEXT TIME your world turns into a winter wonderland of white, add a little color of your own. Add about ten drops of food coloring in any shade you like to about three teaspoons of water in a bowl that it's okay to get dirty. (For each color you want to make, use one bowl.) Carry your colorful "paint" outside.

Pack a four-foot by four-foot section of snow hard and firm to make your canvas. Now, splash that bright color onto the snow using your paint-brushes for an abstract splash. Or paint your favorite characters right on the snow. Be sure to wear older clothes that you can dirty up, because food coloring doesn't wash out of most fabrics.

The Need for Light

What happens when plants don't get light?

What You'll Need:
Weedy patch of
ground,
notebook,
pencil or pen,
board or brick,
large rock (optional)

THIS ACTIVITY *will* harm the plants you observe, so please get permission beforehand. Try to find a weedy patch that hasn't been planted recently. In your notebook, sketch the plants you see in your weed patch. Note their shapes, sizes, and colors. Now cover the weed patch with a board or a brick. Weigh the board down with a rock or brick if you need to. Leave the cover in place for a week. After a week is up, lift the board. What differences do you see? Write down and sketch the changes in your notebook. If you want, put the board back and wait another week. What happens to the plants if they don't get light? How long can they survive without light?

Hot Spots

Where are the hottest spots on a hot day?

What You'll Need:
Outdoor thermometer or soil thermometer, notebook, pencil or pen, miscellaneous materials

I F YOU'RE LIKE most kids, you've tried to walk barefoot on asphalt on a hot day—and regretted it! What you got was a lesson on how some materials capture heat better than others. In this activity, you'll find out how well other materials absorb heat. On a warm, sunny day, go outdoors with a thermometer. Any outdoor thermometer will do, but a soil thermometer (look at a garden center) is useful because it has a strong metal probe that you can stick into the dirt.

Check the air temperature and write it down. Then find different kinds of materials that are in the sun: soil, grass, bark dust, asphalt, metal, water. Hold the bulb end of the thermometer against each material, wait a few minutes, and write down the temperature. Which materials absorbed heat the most? How many were warmer than air? How many were cooler? Which would you rather walk on if *you* were barefoot?

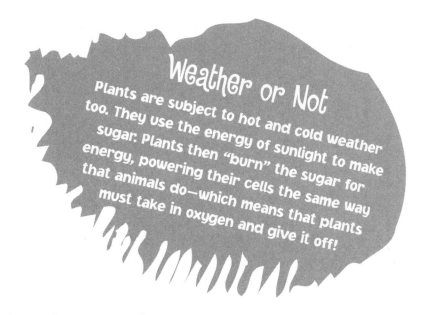

Weather or Not
Plants are subject to hot and cold weather too. They use the energy of sunlight to make sugar. Plants then "burn" the sugar for energy, powering their cells the same way that animals do—which means that plants must take in oxygen and give it off!

The World of Water

One of the coolest things to do on a hot summer day is to put on a T-shirt and swimsuit and just get wet! In this chapter, there's water, water everywhere—to play with, not to drink. You'll discover all sorts of wild games and schemes involving fresh, cool water, whether it's in squirt bottles, balloons, or buckets. You'll even find out how to wash dogs—both real AND stuffed ones!

Wet 'n' Wild Water Race

Get set for some splish-splashing fun! If you like to get wet, this game is definitely up your alley!

What You'll Need:
Friends,
wading pools or
large tubs,
buckets,
water,
paper cups

On YOUR MARK... get wet... go! You and your friends should divide into two even-numbered teams. Place two pools or tubs side by side and fill each one with the same amount of water. Put empty buckets side by side about 30 steps away from the pools. Each team should have its own pool and bucket.

Every player should grab a paper cup and stand in a line beside their bucket. Then... you're off! The first kid in line for each team should run toward their pool, scoop up a cup of water as fast as possible, run back to their bucket, and dump the water in it. Then the next kid in line should make a run for it and do the same thing. The first team to fill its bucket wins the race!

Bouncing Balloons

Do you have what it takes to keep a water balloon in the air? Give this game a try and have a blast!

WHOOSH! You and your friends should each grab a corner of the sheet and place a water balloon in the middle. The object of the game is to bounce the balloon up into the air using the sheet. That may not sound too tough, but the tricky part is catching the balloon in the sheet before it s-p-l-a-t-s on the ground.

Once you and your pals master one balloon, toss another one onto the sheet. How many balloons can you bounce into the air without busting one? You can turn this balloon game into a game of "volleyball" by gathering another four friends together. Use a net or a string to divide a grassy area in two. Then have one group stand on each side of the net. Your team must use the sheet to bounce the balloon over the net. And the team on the other side must catch it with *their* sheet and flip it back over to you. Keep this up until one team drops the balloon. Splash!

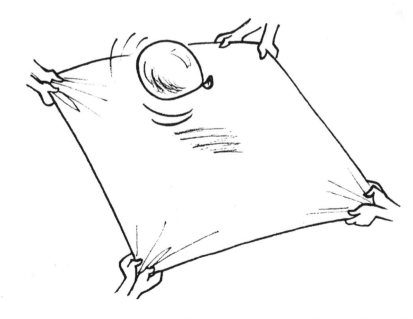

That Sinking Feeling

A penny for your thoughts...or maybe a quarter! Try your luck at this watery game. It's a lot harder than it looks!

What You'll Need:
Bucket,
water,
quarters,
pennies

HERE'S A WAY to have some fun with that handful of change in your piggy bank! Fill a bucket with water and drop a quarter into it. Now take a handful of pennies and drop them into the bucket one by one. Can you drop a penny so that it lands right on top of the quarter at the bottom of the bucket? Keep track of how many tries it takes you to "capture" the quarter.

The Hose Knows

Being a "squirt" can be fun.

What You'll Need:
Water hoses,
rubber play balls,
stopwatch or watch
with second hand

THE NEXT TIME your parents ask you to water the lawn, try this creative approach instead of the usual lawn sprinkler. Gather as many light-weight play balls as you can find—any size or condition will do, even semi-flat or tiny ones.

Now, use a disconnected water hose to make a five-foot circle in the middle of your grassy yard. Place all the balls inside the circle. Take another garden hose (this one connected) in your hands and turn the water on full-blast. Count to three, begin the ball-blasting action, and your friend or parents start the watch. As soon as you clear every ball out of the circle, the clock stops. If you play against friends, whoever has the best time wins. If you play against the clock, see if you can beat your own personal best. Don't forget to clean up the hoses and the balls when you're through.

Balloons Vs. Forks

Splatter your friends just for fun.

What You'll Need:
Water balloons,
hose,
grassy yard,
buckets,
plastic forks,
clean-up trash bag

NOBODY HAS to tell you how much fun water balloon battles can be when the summer temperatures are soaring. But this twist can make the war more interesting. Divide into two even teams. One side will be the offense, one side will be the defense (don't worry; you can switch after the first round). Offense is in charge of launching a water balloon barrage—as many water balloons as you can send soaring in two minutes flat!

Defense is in charge of taking the wet and wild abuse without budging from their line. But here's the twist. Each member of the defensive team is issued a plastic fork. They can reach out and pop the balloon before it hits them, if their aim is quick and true. The team with the most balloons across the defensive line (balloons the forks missed) wins the game. (Don't forget to clean up the balloon bits after you finish your game.) This game is a lot more fun if you fill and bucket at least a hundred water balloons for each side before you start the game.

Flying With Air

Balloons are for more than just playing. On March 1, 1999, Betrand Piccard and Brian Jones became the first people ever to travel around the globe nonstop in a hot-air balloon. Their amazing journey took only 19 days, one hour, and 49 minutes!

Gutter Gators

Float these paper gators downstream.

What You'll Need:

A good rainstorm,
plastic sand bags,
sand (or dirt
or gravel),
thick green paper,
safe scissors,
waterproof marker

THE NEXT TIME it looks like rain, block off a 15-to-20-foot section of your neighborhood gutter with plastic grocery bags filled with sand, dirt, or gravel. All you need is a shallow reservoir of water to give this gator race teeth.

As you wait for the storm to end (and your temporary dam to work), make five to ten three-inch-long paper alligators out of bright green, thick biodegradable paper. Decorate them however you like—use your imagination. Make each one easy to tell from the next. Numbers (in waterproof marker) might be a good idea if your imagination runs a little dry.

Once the rain stops, stand on the sidewalk side of the uphill end of your temporary gutter-lake. STAY OUT OF THE STREET. Have a friend stand on the sidewalk side of the other end. Drop your paper gators in the water, then signal your friend to pull away the dirt-filled bags. Race alongside your waterlogged friends until the stream of water is completely gone. Which gator won the race? Were any held up along the way? Did any mysteriously vanish? You never know where those gutter gators will wind up. But it's always fun to find out.

The Great Summer Melt-off

How long does it take for ice to melt?

What You'll Need:
Partner,
paper cups,
waterproof marker,
ice,
water

In THIS FUN RACE, you and a friend team up to see how quickly you can cause the ice to melt using only your fingers and hands. Mark each paper cup at the halfway point with a waterproof marker. That's how much water MUST remain in the cup to avoid being disqualified in the end.

Now stuff the cup with ice and fill it to the top with water. It's your job to melt the ice faster than your opponent can, using only the swirling action of your fingers and the heat of your hands to make it happen. And remember, the cup must remain at least half full or you're out of the competition.

Ice Shot

Blow your friends away with this fun test of oral accuracy.

What You'll Need:
Paper,
washable markers,
tape,
drinking straws,
finely crushed ice

SOME ANCIENT TRIBES used blow guns to hunt for food for their families. Now that we have grocery stores to keep that covered, why not use the power of your breath for some wild and watery fun?

Make targets out of paper and color them with washable markers. Make sure nothing is left white. Now tape your targets to a fence post and back away at least ten paces. Using an ordinary drinking straw as your blow gun and tiny pieces of crushed ice as your "darts," shoot for those targets with all the hot air you can muster. Set a time limit for each player, then check your target for watery smear marks—dead-on hits of ice. The person with the most hits wins the round.

Wade and Wonder

Let your fingers guess the watery secrets.

What You'll Need:
Wading pool, at least ten floating toys, blindfold

SPLASHING AROUND in a wading pool is fun, but you can only splash so long. If your energy runs out before the heat fades, try this with a partner. Drop ten to twenty floating toys in the pool. Blindfold one player while the other acts as a guide. One by one, the guide should hand the toys to the blindfolded one. Can he or she guess which toy is which? Keep track of how many he or she gets right. Now switch places, and see how well you do.

What's in There?

Who lives in your lakes and streams?

What You'll Need:
Sand shovel and pail, mesh or cheesecloth, rubber flip-flop shoes

MOST OF US think we have a pretty good idea of what lives in our local streams and lakesides. But do we really have a clue? Dig in to find out. The next time you head for the wilderness, bring a bucket, a sand shovel, some cheesecloth or very fine mesh, and an adventurous mind. Wearing rubber flip-flops for safety (just in case something sharp is in the murky water), wade a few inches into the water.

Dig just an inch or so into the dirt or gravel at the bottom of the water and fill your bucket halfway, including a little lake or river water in the mix. Now wade back to the edge. Scoop about a cup full of the dirt and water onto your mesh or cheesecloth, allowing the water to sift through. What do you see? Maybe nothing—but maybe a tiny watery world you never knew existed. You'll have to dig in to find out.

Water Balloon Launch

Send water balloons sailing through the air.

What You'll Need:
Adult,
awl or drill,
large plastic funnel,
12 feet of rubber
tubing,
dozens of water
balloons,
two buckets,
plastic garbage
can lids

To make a launcher, have an adult use an awl or drill to make four holes in the upper rim of a large plastic funnel and cut the rubber tubing into two equal lengths. Tie an end of the tubing to each of the four holes so that the funnel has two big loops of tube coming from each side.

Firing the launcher requires three people. Have two people hold the loops, one on each side, with their arms in the air and the launcher stretched between them. The third person puts a water balloon in the funnel and pulls back on the funnel as far as it will go and touches it to the ground, then releases it, sending the balloon flying.

To play water balloon battleship, you'll need two launchers and two buckets of water balloons. Divide the players into two teams with at least four players per team. Three "cannoneers" operate the launcher and the fourth, the "powder monkey," fetches the water balloons. Extra players can carry plastic garbage can lids to protect their teammates. Each bucket of balloons should be behind the team and off to the side.

At a signal, the powder monkeys run and fetch one water balloon at a time for their team. Teams fire balloons as fast as they can. A person hit directly is "wounded" and must move around on one leg only. A second "hit" puts the player out of the game for an agreed-on period of time. You can vary the rules according to the number of players and how well they play. A heavy splash might count as a "wound" if a team's aim is not good.

Bubble Pie

Line up for soapy fun.

What You'll Need:
Play area,
four buckets,
liquid dish soap,
hose and water,
aluminum pie tins

THIS WET and wacky relay is made for fun in the summer sun. Fill two big buckets with sudsy, soapy water. Put two empty buckets on the opposite end of the playing field. Divide into two teams, each lined up behind the soapy bucket. The leader in each line holds the empty pie tin. When the whistle blows, fill the pie tin with soapy water and head for the opposite end of the field. Dump what's left of your "pie" in the empty bucket and run back to your line. Pass the empty pie pan to the next person in line, then head for the back of the line. That person repeats the whole process, which continues until everyone in the line has had a turn. The team with the most bubbly water in the bucket at the other end of the field claims the bubble championship.

Big Bubble

It takes a lot of practice to blow a big bubble. But even if you practiced morning 'til night, it'd be pretty tough to beat David Stein, who mixed up his own bubble mixture and then created a balloon 50 feet long. That's nearly as long as two school buses placed end to end!

Water Balloon Cut-up

Slice into some wet and wild action.

What You'll Need:
Water balloons,
hose and water,
paper plates,
plastic knives

IF YOU'VE EVER tried to cut up a polish sausage, you'll know this game—except that the weenie you're about to carve is a water balloon. And the minute you cut into the "meat," you get wonderfully wet. Fill your paper plate with water weenies (long, thin balloons filled with cool water from the hose). Take your plastic butter knife in hand and wait for the signal to start (have someone blow a whistle or just say "Go!"). The first person to "carve" five "weenies" wins the race. No one to compete against? Race the clock instead. Set your best time, then see if you can beat it. A hint: Have the water balloons (lots of them, at least 15 for each player) filled before you start the game.

Squirt Bottle Barber

Wash away your whiskers.

What You'll Need:
Squirt bottles,
water,
goggles,
shaving cream

PLAYING WITH Dad's shaving cream is pretty hard to resist. In this game, it's a MUST. Divide into pairs and get ready for a close shave. One player in each team holds a squirt bottle full of clean, cool water. The other slips into swimmer's goggles and spreads shaving cream all over the lower half of their face. When the "go" signal sounds, the "barber" begins to squirt the face of his partner, from a distance of about five feet, trying to wash away any sign of shaving foam. The first team with a clean shave wins the race.

Egg Roll

Crack open a great new egg-sperience.

What You'll Need:
Plastic Easter eggs, water bottles or hoses, level playing field

TEST THE POWER of water—squirt bottles or hoses—with this fun relay. Each player has their own plastic Easter egg (a different color for each, just to keep things straight). The first person in line places their egg on the ground and grabs the team hose or water bottle. When the starter says "go," begin to move the egg down the playing field, towards the finish line, using only the stream of water from your hose or water bottle. Once your egg crosses that line, head back to your team and pass the hose or squirter. The first team to move all their colored eggs across the line wins.

Water on the Move

Find out what happens to the water that plants take in through their roots.

What You'll Need:
Easy-to-reach tree branch with leaves, clear plastic bag (large enough to cover several leaves), string, measuring spoons

THE "PLUMBING SYSTEM" of trees and other plants carries water on a one-way trip from roots to leaves. Evaporation of water on the surface of the leaves is one force that helps move the water. To see this, try a simple experiment. On a sunny morning, find a tree branch that you can reach easily. Cover a cluster of leaves with a plastic bag and tie the bag in place with string. Leave in place until evening.

When you return, notice how much water has collected in the bag. Remove the bag, being careful not to spill any water. Gently dip the water out by teaspoons. How much water did the leaves give off in one day? Divide this amount by the number of leaves in the bag to find out how much one single leaf gives off. Just for fun, estimate how many leaves are on the tree, then multiply by the amount of water one single leaf gave off. How much water did the tree give off in a day?

Stuffy Wash Playoff

Fast is first when you shampoo plush pets.

What You'll Need:
Stuffed animals,
stopwatch,
shampoo,
buckets,
hose and water

How LONG does it take to give a pet a bath? Gather all your friends and their stuffed animals in your backyard to find out.

Each player has their own fabric friend. When the clock starts, get to work. Wet and soap that stuffy. Make sure the entire animal is covered in suds, then hose it down and check your time. The quickest groomer wins the race.

Spoon Spill

Sometimes, soggy rules supreme.

What You'll Need:
Teaspoons,
dark colored
construction paper,
paper cups

When you spill water on your favorite drawing, it's no fun. But in this game, when you spill water—spoon by spoon—on a piece of construction paper, it's a race to the wettest! Each player gets a teaspoon, a paper cup of water, and 60 seconds. Whoever gets their piece of paper the wettest from a distance of three feet in just one minute wins the game. But remember, no fair tossing your whole cup of H_2O. The idea is to win this race one spoon at a time. One hint: Be sure to use construction paper. It shows (and absorbs) water better than other kinds of paper.

Spoon It Up!

How long does it take to fill a bowl the old-fashioned way?

What You'll Need:
Empty bowl,
water-filled bowl,
large spoon,
stopwatch or watch
with a second hand

THERE WAS A TIME when farmers had to carry buckets of water from rivers or ponds to water their crops. Bucket by bucket, they carried the load. Want a quick and crazy way to appreciate that kind of work? See how long it takes to move a bowl full of water into an empty bowl—carrying just one spoonful at a time.

Set two bowls on opposite sides of a yard or small playing field. As soon as the stopwatch starts, begin to transport water from a full bowl to an empty bowl one spoon at a time. Do your best not to spill as you go. Then throw your hands over your head when your mission is complete. The timer with the second hand can tell you just how long it took. Your powers of reason will tell you how much longer it might take to irrigate a plot of old farming acreage, one bucket at a time.

How Cold Is It?

Take a dip to determine temperatures.

What You'll Need:
Bowl of water,
ice,
thermometer,
bare feet,
notebook,
pencil or pen

WE KNOW the average healthy human body maintains a temperature of about 98.6 degrees. But can our bodies accurately read temperatures lower than that? Play this "dippy" game to find out. On a warm day, sit outside and dip a naked toe into a bowl of water and make a guess at what temperature the water actually is. Measure the real temperature with a thermometer and write it beside your guess. Now add some ice to the bowl and guess again. Measure the correct temperature and write both figures down. Now carefully add warm water to the ice water (making sure it's not too hot to touch), stick your toe in, and repeat the process. See if your body even comes close to guessing the correct temperatures.

Dog Wash

95

Polished poochy could mean a pocket full of cash.

What You'll Need:
Cheap no-name baby shampoo, water, plastic bucket, old towels

WANT TO TRY a wet and wild moneymaker when the summer months finally hit? Check out the fun and profit possible in washing your neighborhood's pet dogs. Slip into your swimsuit, then let your neighbors know you and a partner will bathe dogs for just $3 a head. Start with the pups in your own backyards.

Have one partner gently hold the dog while the other washes. First, wet the dog down, carefully avoiding getting water in its ears or eyes. Pour about two tablespoons of generic baby shampoo into your wet hands and rub them together to make a soap and water paste. Now apply it to the dog's back and chest. Work up a good lather, again, careful of the eyes and ears. Hose all the soap from the dog's body as you rub (be sure that every trace rinses away). Towel excess water off the dog and collect your cash!

Where's the Water?
Water covers three-quarters of the planet earth, but 97% of that water is salt water (which we can't drink or wash in). Two-thirds of the earth's fresh water is frozen in ice caps and glaciers, so it is also impossible for most of us to use.

Water Balloon Weigh-In

Guess well or prepare to be soaked.

What You'll Need:
Balloons,
water,
fruit scale or
digital scale,
paper,
pencil or pen

Can you guess how much that swollen water balloon your friend is holding actually weighs? Let's hope so, because if you can't guess the weight of the water, you'll be wearing it soon enough. First, fill at least two water balloons for each person playing the game. Then appoint one person scorekeeper. It's up to the scorekeeper to write down the other players' guesses and confirm the actual weight once the balloon is placed on the fruit scale. If the person guessing is within five ounces, he's spared. If not, his opponent gets to break the balloon in question over his rival's head. The person with the most correct answers (and the driest clothing) wins.

Hole-y Hose

Fix those leaks—fast.

What You'll Need:
Old garden hose,
hammer,
nail,
adult help,
duct tape,
stopwatch (optional)

Have your folks decided that old, leaky garden hose has got to go? Don't let them toss it until you try this crazy game. Before the hose lands in the trash heap, carefully take a hammer and a nail to it, sinking holes ever few inches down the length. Now attach that hose to an ordinary water spigot and get ready to let 'er rip.

Your assignment is to try and repair the hose with duct tape while water is gushing out of the holes. You can time yourself if you like. Be prepared: It's nearly impossible to properly duct-tape the holes shut. But it's great fun giving the impossible a wet and wacky try. NOTE: Make sure you put the nail and hammer away before you begin the game. The only thing you want punctured in this adventure is the hose, not bare feet, elbows, or knees.

Testing PFDs

A PFD is a Personal Flotation Device.
Test one out in a pool and see how it works!

What You'll Need:

Use of a pool,
any life jackets
or other PFDs in
your household,
adult help

LIFE JACKETS and other personal flotation devices (PFDs) are meant to keep you afloat if you accidentally fall into the water. However, they only work if you actually wear them properly. Don't think you can grab one quickly and put it on if your boat capsizes. You never know what will happen in an accident! If you've never tried out a PFD before, do so before you go boating.

Get permission to try a life vest in a swimming pool. First, put the life vest on over a swim suit. Have an adult help you adjust the straps so it fits snugly. Then, with an adult in the pool to help you in case something goes wrong, jump in the pool and see what happens!

If the vest feels uncomfortable, or if it makes you float awkwardly, adjust the straps or try a different size or style. Once you find a vest that fits, test it out. Then put on clothes you would wear if you were boating or playing or fishing near open water. Put the life vest on over your clothes, adjust the straps, and jump in the pool. How does it feel? Will the vest keep you afloat with your clothes on? Knowing what it's like to float in a life vest will make things easier later.

Making Rainbows

You don't have to wait for a rainy day to see rainbows!

What You'll Need:
Prism,
spray nozzle,
hose,
glass baking dish,
water, white paper,
unbreakable mirror,
two straight sticks,
string,
chandelier crystals
or faceted beads,
fishing line

RAINBOWS ARE made when white light is broken up into its many colors. A glass prism can make this happen, but plain water can, too! The rainbows you see in the sky are made when sunlight passes through raindrops. Even without rain, you can try some of these fun rainbow-makers.

PRISMS: Toy and science stores sell inexpensive plastic prisms. Hold the prism in a beam of light and tilt it until you can see a rainbow on any nearby flat surface.

WATER SPRAY: On a bright, sunny day, attach a spray nozzle to a hose and turn on the water. Adjust the nozzle to make a fine, misty spray. Turn it until the sunlight shines through the mist and makes rainbows.

MIRROR: Fill a glass baking dish with water and set it on a flat surface outdoors. Position it near a light-colored wall or hold up a large sheet of white paper. Put an unbreakable mirror in the water and tilt it so that it reflects sunlight onto the wall or the paper. You should see ripply, watery rainbows on the paper.

RAINBOW MOBILE: Tie two straight sticks together to form an "X." Hang faceted glass or plastic beads from it using fishing line. If you have crystals, hang some from a chandelier on the mobile as well. Hang the mobile up in a window where sunlight can shine through. You'll see rainbows on the opposite wall.

Water Sprayers

Cool off with a yard full of homemade sprinklers.

What You'll Need:

Strong stake or
old broomstick,
hammer
(get adult help),
18-inch length of
rubber tubing,
hose and faucet,
old rubber glove,
tin can,
nail,
string

Running through the sprinkler on a hot day is a great way to cool down, but it's even more fun when you can make your own fun sprinklers. If you have enough hoses and faucets, you can set up these water sprayers and a few sprinklers in your yard. Invite your friends over for a water party!

WATER WHIP: Drive a stake or an old broomstick into the ground. Take a piece of rubber tubing at least one-half inch in diameter and stretch one end over the end of a garden hose. Tie the hose to the stake so that the rubber tubing can flap freely at the top. Turn on the water, and adjust the height of the hose and the water pressure until the tubing waves around on its own, spraying water as it goes.

WATER HAND: Poke holes in the fingertips of an old rubber glove, such as a dish-washing glove. Tie the cuff of the glove tightly over the end of a hose. Fasten the water hand to a stake so it sprays upright, or drape the hose over a tree branch to make a "handy" shower!

TIN CAN SHOWER: Use a nail to punch holes around the bottom edge of a large tin can. Punch two more holes at the top and insert a string to hang the can from a branch. Fill the can with water. As water sprays out through the holes, the can will spin!

Open-Air Science

If you think science lessons belong in the classroom, think again! This chapter is full of science activities you can do in the park, playground, or your backyard. When you try these activities out, start thinking like a scientist. Read the activity. Make a hypothesis—that is, a prediction about what's going to happen. Carry out the activity. Was your hypothesis correct or incorrect? Either way you win, because you've learned something!

Ant Hill Horde

101

Ancient finds, tiny heroes.

What You'll Need:
Gardening gloves, insect repellent, tiny jar with lid or cloth bag

PALEONTOLOGISTS know ants can be the masters of any prehistoric dig. They spend hours and hours of each day tunneling through the earth, improving their habitats. As they dig, they often find chunks of material that we might miss digging on our own.

As a result, paleontologists know to search the dirt piles of ants carefully for tiny prehistoric bits. For instance, tiny teeth are common in certain fossil-rich areas like Wyoming and Montana.

So the next time you see an ant hill, don't stomp it! Study it! Put on your best gardening gloves, use insect repellent to keep you safe, and start looking. You just might find some fossil teeth of your own. Remember to ask the owner of the land permission to search for fossils first. And if you are on public land, give your discovery to a scientist. Keeping fossils found on public land is almost always against the law.

Fossil Finds

Nature makes a lasting impression.

What You'll Need:
Sidewalks,
paper,
crayons

WE THINK OF FOSSILS as ancient reminders captured in stone. But modern fossils are everywhere, and are as close as the sidewalks under your feet. The next time you take a walk, keep your eyes on the cement to make a few modern-day fossil finds. The "fossil" could be an imprint from a shoe, the pecking of a persistent bird, or a chip made by some unseen tool. For extra fun, bring along paper and a crayon to make rubbings of what you discover. Just lay the paper over the "fossil" and rub a crayon across the spot to make an exact "copy" of the image on your page.

Things Pan Out

Go for the gold.

What You'll Need:
Old pie pan,
cheesecloth,
fine mesh strainer,
riverside

THOUSANDS OF gold miners searched for their fortunes during the 1800s. Some of them went deep into caves to search for riches. Some panned for the gold they found. You can try your hand at gold panning too, using these easy tips.

Gather an old pie or cake pan, a piece of fine cheesecloth, and a metal mesh strainer and head for a riverside. First, gather a scoop of riverbed dirt in a metal strainer. Rinse the finer dirt from the scoop using river water, with the cake pan just beneath the strainer. That cake pan catches the finer dirt and metal that sifts through the strainer. Now strain *that* finer material through cheesecloth, again using river water. See any golden flakes? You might have struck gold, and even fool's gold is fun.

River Rock Mystery

Well-rounded stones and how they got that way.

What You'll Need:
Bucket,
stream or riverbed

SCOOP UP A BUCKET of river rocks and sand and what will you find? Smooth, rounded stones, more often than not. Examine a few of the stones, then imagine the journeys they've made downstream and figure out WHY they're more rounded than their mountainside friends. Once you've found some smooth rocks, see if you can follow their trail to find out how they got to the river and where they came from. Go up the gravel paths, to the high ridges and mountain sides. It's always interesting to imagine how a stone got where it is and how it came to look the way it does.

Layers of Time

Stripes of mystery revealed.

What You'll Need:
Paper,
colored pencils
or crayons,
self-addressed
stamped envelope

HAVE YOU EVER noticed the ribbons of colors that run throughout some roadside cliffs? Next time you pass one of these colorful rock formations, stop and make a sketch. Be as careful and accurate with colors as you can. Once you've finished your sketch, send a color copy of the drawing, along with its exact location, to the U.S. Geological Survey office and a local University geology department or local natural history museum asking what the colors mean. Be sure to enclose a self-addressed stamped envelope with your letter so that the scientists can write back about what they see between your colorful lines. You'll learn a lot about geology and ancient history.

Rocky Rainbow

How many colors can you find in your own backyard?

What You'll Need:
Bag or plastic jar for collection, glue or duct tape, posterboard

NATURE HAS created literally hundreds of differently colored rocks. Many of them can be found in your own yard. When you're feeling ready to explore, see how many different tones you can discover and collect in a single day's geological expedition. If you want, you can mount the stones on a piece of posterboard. Just for fun, take your poster to a nearby natural history museum or geology professor. Ask why your rock specimens are the color they are. You might be fascinated to discover what chemicals work to give a rock its hue.

Fossil Junior

Study how fossils begin.

What You'll Need:
Small garden shovel, work gloves, old toothbrush

BEFORE FOSSILS turn to stone, they rest in dirt. Search for fossils-in-the-making to help understand how the process actually works. First, ask your parents' permission before you dig in any part of their landscaped yard. Once you have the green light, dig carefully with a small work shovel and gloves.

If you find a leaf or dead bug embedded in the soil, use an old toothbrush to carefully remove excess dirt from the "fossil." See if you can gently remove the bug or plant. Is there an impression left where the bug once was? Now imagine—left undisturbed, that very bug might have been transformed into a fossil millions of years into the future. See how the future is connected to the past?

Sandstone Carving

Written in stone.

What You'll Need:
Sandstone,
screwdriver or
hammer and nail,
parental supervision

ANCIENT PEOPLES often carved their favorite stories into the faces of giant rocks. They left their history behind for us to study and explore. You can express yourself in stone too if you select the rock carefully. Be sure to ask before you carve and have an adult help you choose the right tools. Once you have permission, take a screwdriver or a hammer and nail. Carefully chisel your first initial into the side of the stone. Check back in a week, a month, and even a year to see if your carving has withstood the test of time. Wind and blowing dirt can blast your mark from the stone in a process called erosion.

Fun Fake Fossils

Even the fossils you make today can teach you about the past.

What You'll Need:
Pie pan, sand, water,
chicken bones, twigs,
shells, leaves,
cooking oil,
plaster of Paris,
coffee (optional)

HOW DID CREATURES that lived thousands—even millions—of years ago leave fossils that we discover today? This fun experiment will help you understand. Fill a pie pan with fine-grain sand. Add a little water and softly pat down flat and smooth. Now coat your favorite bones, twigs, shells, or leaves with cooking oil. Firmly press them into the soil, leaving a clear, clean impression. Once you've made your mark, remove the bone or shell and fill the pan with plaster of Paris. If you want a more authentic-looking fossil, use strong, dark coffee instead of water to mix your plaster. Once the plaster is completely dry (overnight should be plenty of time unless the weather is especially humid), lift it out of the sand and examine the fossil imprints now standing up off the plaster face. That will give you an idea of how some fossils are formed.

How High is That Hill?

Use a simple surveying tool to measure the height of any slope.

What You'll Need:
Clear plastic jar,
waterproof marker,
a partner,
tape measure,
paper, pen,
calculator

To MEASURE the height of a slope, you'll need a tool called a level. Make a simple level by filling a jar about a third of the way with water. Put it on a flat table and, with a waterproof marker, make a ring around the jar at the water level. Then have your partner use a tape measure to measure the height from the floor to your eyes. Write this measurement down. Call this your "eye-level distance."

Stand at the bottom of the slope and hold the jar so that the water level is even with the ring on the jar. Look through the jar, across the surface of the water, and have your partner stand at the point on the hill that you can see across the water. Your partner is now standing one eye-level distance above you.

Now go up the hill and stand by your partner. Look across the level water again and have your partner move to the next point you can see on the hill. Your partner is now two eye-level distances up the hill. Continue doing this until your partner is on the top of the hill. Then multiply the number of eye-level distances you measured out by the number of inches from the floor to your eyes. This will tell you how many inches high the hill is. Divide by 12 to find out how many *feet* high it is.

Rockhounder's Scavenger Hunt

Rock steady with this geologic search.

What You'll Need:
List of local rocks and descriptions, paper bags, markers, partners

ROCKHOUNDS ARE people always on the prowl for new kinds of rocks. Become a quick expert on your area's most common rocks with this hunt. Ask your local librarian for books on rocks common to your hometown. Make a list of those rocks—including descriptions of them—and make photocopies while you're at the library. Once you get that list home, give it to your friends along with ordinary brown paper bags. Now team up in pairs and head out to find as many of those ordinary rocks as you can. The team with the most rocks gets to talk about their adventure first.

Rock and Roll

Does shape affect how a rock rolls? You decide.

What You'll Need:
Differently shaped rocks, hillside, watch with second hand, paper, pen

PICK SIX DIFFERENTLY shaped rocks of about the same size and weight. One might be rounded, one might be flat on one side, and one might be almost square or totally flat. One by one, release these rocks at the top of a steep hill and time how long each takes to roll to the bottom. Try to predict which rocks you think will move the fastest before letting them go. Compare your times and see how close your predictions came to being correct.

City Fossil Hunt

Look carefully to find fossils right in the middle of the city!

What You'll Need:
Magnifying glass,
notebook,
pen or pencil

Fossils are made when animals or plants are trapped in sediment (such as mud, wet sand, or river silt). This may happen when a leaf falls on a mud flat or even if a flood sweeps away a herd of animals. If conditions are right, minerals from the sediments slowly replace the material in the bones of the animals. Plant parts and animal parts can leave imprints in mud that dry and can be preserved for thousands of years. Eventually the sediments may turn to rock, such as sandstone, shale, limestone, or slate. Under heat and pressure, sedimentary rocks may change into metamorphic rocks such as marble.

Sometimes, sedimentary and metamorphic rocks are used to make buildings. Take a walk around your city and hunt for buildings using rocks in their construction. The rocks used most often are granite and marble. Granite was formed from hardened lava, so you won't find fossils in it. It's rare to find fossils in metamorphic rock, but observe them closely anyway. You may find a few fossils of sea shells stretched and deformed along with the rock! If you can find a building that uses sedimentary rocks, you may be in luck. Look carefully for the remains of ancient creatures. They may be small, so use your magnifying glass to hunt for tiny shells. Keep track of your findings.

Slide Friction

Learn about the force of friction and how it is reduced.

What You'll Need:
Playground slide, items to be tested (toys with wheels, wooden blocks, rocks), stopwatch, partner, waxed paper, water

FRICTION IS A FORCE that stops motion. If there were no friction in the world, anything that starts moving in one direction would never stop. If you slide a wooden block across a floor, friction between the block and the floor makes the block stop. In this activity, you'll find out how friction affects an object and how friction can be reduced. Lay out your items to be tested and decide which ones will go down the slide the fastest. Test each item one at a time. With your stopwatch ready, have your partner hold one item at the top of the slide and release it on your signal. See how long it takes for the item to reach the bottom. Which objects go the fastest? What qualities made them move faster than others?

Now, take one of the objects and rub the bottom of it with waxed paper. See how long it takes for it to reach the bottom of the slide. Try setting it on a square of waxed paper and see if *that* reduces friction. Wet the slide and see what effect water has. Will the items move faster or slower? Does the amount of water matter?

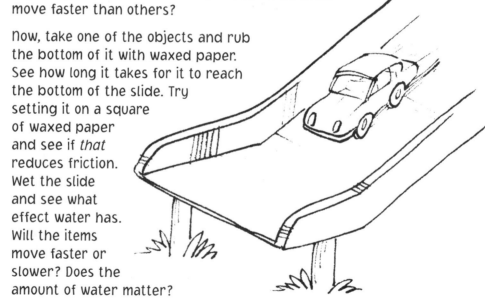

How Hard Is It?

If you think all rocks are alike, think again.

What You'll Need:
Safety goggles,
gloves,
different kinds
of rocks,
large nail,
small hammer

ALL ROCKS SEEM the same. But are they? Not by a long shot. One swing of a small hammer will tell you that some rocks are meant to last and some are meant to turn to sand. Before you start this activity, be sure to ask permission from your parents. Wear gloves and safety goggles to protect your eyes. (Rock splinters can cause injuries if you're not careful.) Once you have permission, and have put the goggles over your eyes, carefully place the point of an ordinary nail in the center of a rock. Using the hammer, drive the nail in. Does the rock split in half? Does it chip? Does it refuse to crack? How it reacts to the pounding will tell you a little about how long it might last.

Swing on a Pendulum

Discover the physics of a pendulum on the playground swing.

What You'll Need:
Swing set,
partner, stopwatch

YOU PROBABLY KNOW that the harder you pump on a swing, the higher you go. You probably feel like you're going faster, too. But how does this affect the swing's periodicity—that is, does the swing actually go back and forth more times per minute? Sit in a swing and have your partner push you gently. Time how many times you go back and forth in one minute. Don't pump the swing. Just let it go on its own. You partner can use a stopwatch to time precisely one minute while you count. Next, have your partner push you as hard as possible. Again, don't pump the swing. Count how many times you go back and forth in one minute. Is it any different? Now try the same experiment, but pump the swing yourself. Does adding a force affect the periodicity of the swing?

See-Saw Balance

Turn a see-saw into a balance and find out how scales work.

What You'll Need:
See-saw,
two or more
partners

Have you ever wondered how the scale at the doctor's office works? How can small weights balance your own larger weight? Use a see-saw to find out. Before you begin, however, agree that no one will jump off the see-saw while another person is sitting on it. The sudden jolt can cause serious injury. First, sit on one end of the see-saw and have a partner sit on the other end. Is the see-saw balanced? Have the heavier person move toward the middle of the see-saw until it balances. Notice that neither of you changed your weight; only your *position* changed.

Now have two people sit on one side of the see-saw and one person on the other. Decide together how to move people so that the see-saw becomes level. Should the two people move to the middle, or should the single person move?

Step on It

Make walkways for your garden.

What You'll Need:
Large flat rocks

Another way to use the larger stones you discover on your geologic journeys is to make them into stepping stones for your gardens, yard or flowerbeds—especially to help you make a safe path to where you keep the garden hose. Just take your flat, heavy stones and put them about six inches apart on a trail, either between rows in your garden or in flowerbeds near the spigot for the hose.

Noise Pollution

noise is one pollution that is often overlooked.

What You'll Need:
Tape recorder
(optional)

WALK AROUND your neighborhood and listen for as many sounds as possible: cars, trucks, birds, dogs, lawn mowers, and all other noises. How many of these sounds do you normally notice? How many do you usually ignore? You may be so used to the noises that you don't notice them anymore. If you like, take a tape recorder with you as you listen. Record as many sounds as you can find.

Make recordings of any sounds that you consider noise pollution. Is your neighborhood too loud? Use your memory (or your tape recorder) to remember the types of noises that bothered you the most. Then decide what you can do about them. Start with the noises that your own household produces. Some communities have banned leaf blowers because they are too noisy and cause pollution. If you have a leaf blower, consider using a broom to clean your sidewalks and a rake to collect leaves from your yard. It takes about the same time and doesn't take that much effort. Gas-powered lawn mowers are also very noisy. Some people use push mowers instead—and get their exercise while they mow! Talk to your neighbors about ways you are reducing noise pollution. Maybe they'll follow your example.

Crunch!

Talk about noise! Astronomers agree that the most common feature in the solar system is the impact crater (created by striking comets and meteors). Entire planets, moons, and asteroids are covered with them.

 # Spinning Swings

How do ice skaters spin so fast? Find out on a playground swing.

What You'll Need:
Playground swing,
partner,
stopwatch

Only do this activity if your parents say it's okay to get a little dizzy! Sit on the swing and have your partner turn you slowly around and around until the swing is wound up tightly. Have a stopwatch ready, and when your partner lets go, time how long it takes for the swing to unwind. Next, try the same thing with your arms and legs stretched out as far as they will go. This puts some of your weight away from the center of mass. Time how long it takes for the swing to unwind.

Now, do the same thing but pull your arms and legs in close to your body. This brings all your weight close to your center. Did you go faster this time? Next time you see skaters on television or in a show, watch how they hold their arms when they spin. The closer their arms are to their bodies, the faster they can whirl.

 # Curve Balls

Does a curve ball *really* curve in flight?

What You'll Need:
Ping-pong ball,
waterproof marker,
playing field marked
with straight lines
(like a baseball
diamond),
paper towel tube

This activity requires either a windless day or a school gymnasium (or other large indoor space). To prepare, color one half of the ping-pong ball with the marker. This will help you see what happens to it in flight. Stand on a marked line on the playing field or gym and try to throw the ping-pong ball straight down the line. Throw it in such a way that you don't make the ball spin at all. What path does the ball take?

Now, put the ball in one end of the paper tube. Holding the other end, fling the ball out of the tube, trying to throw it straight. What path does it take now? Try this several times. You should see the ball spin. The axis of the spin is perpendicular to the flight path of the ball. The spin actually changes the path of the ball and makes it fly in a curve!

Be a Sound Detective

Does sound travel better through some materials than others? Find out for yourself!

What You'll Need:
A partner

I**F YOU'VE EVER** watched old westerns, you may have seen a character put one ear to the ground and announce that the cavalry was coming, or listen to the rail of a train track and know that a train was on its way. Does this really work? To find out, go to a playground with a partner on a warm day. Have your partner go to the other side of the playground, then run back. Raise your hand as soon as you can hear the sound of your partner's running feet. Now have your partner run across the playground again, but this time put your ear to the ground. See if you can hear your partner's feet sooner.

When it's not too hot or too cold, find a long, metal object such as a chain-link fence post (watch out for loose metal). Stand at one end and have your partner tap the post. Then put your ear to the rail and have your partner tap again. Does it sound different? Does it seem louder? Try the same experiment with the materials around you. Does sound travel better through some materials than others? Do some materials muffle sound?

Sound in the Sea

Sound travels well through water. How fast it travels depends mostly on the water's temperature. Whales take advantage of different temperature layers in the oceans to call to other whales who may be as far as hundreds of miles away!

Sound waves are waves of energy that move the molecules of the substance they travel through. Air molecules are much farther apart than the molecules of solid metal. Consider the density of the material (that is, how close together the molecules are) as you try to figure out why sound would move through metal better than through air.

Locating Echoes

Can you find good echoes in your community?

What You'll Need:
Your senses

ECHOES ARE sound waves that begin in one place, bounce off an object, and can be heard in another place. How far away must you be from an object to hear an echo? What kinds of objects produce echoes? Find a large building or a huge wall near your home. (Make sure the loud noises won't disturb anyone.) Shout "Echo!" at the wall and listen for an echo. Back away from the wall a few steps at a time and see how far away you must be before you hear an echo. Try the same activity near a large tree and see what happens. Do you hear an echo, or does the shape of the tree muffle the sound? Try making echoes in different areas around your neighborhood and record the best places to hear them.

Sound Barriers

Find out how sound can be stopped.

What You'll Need:
A partner

GO INTO YOUR backyard and stand about as far from your partner as your house is wide. (That should be about 30 feet or so.) Try to talk to one another. As long as there is nothing between you and your partner, you should be able to hear one another fairly well, though you may have to raise your voice a little. Now stand on one side of a house while your partner stands on the other side. Try to shout something to your partner and see if you can be heard clearly. Have your partner shout something at you. What happened? You may have heard something, but perhaps you could not make out what your partner was saying. Was the sound weak and distorted? Try the same experiment with a wall between you and your partner. Try it with a fence, a window, a blanket, and other types of barriers. Does the thickness of the barrier matter?

Rock Garden

This garden really ROCKS!

What You'll Need:
Decorative rocks,
flowerbed

GARDENERS in many lands use rocks in their flowerbeds for decoration. You can do the same. If you find larger rocks that you'd like to add to your collection, why not consider a rock garden in your own back-yard? (Before you start, be sure you ask permission before you collect rocks on *any* private or public property.) Clear a nice, flat part of your flowerbed, removing all weeds and grasses. Now arrange some of your favorite bigger rocks on the soil. Keep the bigger rocks towards the back of the bed, the smaller towards the front (so you can see them all clearly). If you like, add some tiny gravel to complete the stoney look.

Can Rocks Float?

Even a rock can be full of surprises.

What You'll Need:
Pumice,
bucket or bowl
of water

MOST ROCKS DROP with a "kerplop" to the bottom of a stream or a lake (or any body of water). But one volcanic rock won't sink like a stone when tossed into the drink. In fact, it will float and bob at the top. Don't believe it? Check out an air-filled rock called pumice, which is created by volcanic activity. It looks different from other rocks, and even feels light when you hold it in your hand, but it's a genuine rock and a must for any rock collector. Try to sink it in a bucket. It will float!

The Expansive Sky

Lie on your back in the grass and look up at the sky. What do you see? Clouds? Stars? A rainbow? What you'll see depends not only upon the time of day, but the time of year as well. Some activities in this chapter will have you gazing at the day or night sky. Others are crafts and simulations that will help you understand what you see. As you try these activities, you'll join the ranks of thousands of amateur astronomers still making important contributions to the science. Who knows what *you* could discover?

As Clouds Roll By

Build this cloud chaser and *see* the wind blow!

What You'll Need:
Piece of cardboard,
marker,
tape,
small mirror,
compass

Swoooosh! There goes the wind...and now you can see it! First, mark out north, south, east, and west on the outside edge of a piece of cardboard. Include other directions, like northeast, if you like. Then tape a small mirror to the cardboard so that the compass directions form a circle around the mirror. Now you're ready to chase the wind!

Place your cloud chaser on the ground so it faces north. You can do this by matching north on your cloud chaser with north on your compass. Lie next to your cloud chaser and watch the reflection of the clouds in the mirror. Once you see which way the clouds are moving, you'll know that's the same direction that the wind is blowing.

Solar-Powered Pictures

Here is a way to make shadow pictures from sunlight.

What You'll Need:

Flat objects like keys, leaves, and flowers, safe scissors, stiff cardboard, flat pan, glass baking dish or sheet of clear acrylic, light-sensitive paper (such as Sunprint brand paper)

FIRST, ASSEMBLE the materials you want to make prints from. Grass, leaves, and flowers make good prints. You can also look around the house for small objects such as keys, paper clips, and shaped erasers. Cut a sheet of stiff cardboard a little larger than the printing paper. In a dim place, lay your objects on the cardboard and decide how to arrange them. Then set the objects aside and make a print.

Pour water in a flat pan and have it ready to develop your prints. Open the package of light-sensitive paper and remove one sheet. Lay the sheet on the cardboard, then arrange your objects on the paper. Set the glass baking dish or clear acrylic on the paper. Lift the whole stack and set in bright sun for three to five minutes. Remove the paper and soak in the water for about one minute. Set your print in a dry, shady place to dry. You will see white shadows on a blue background.

Frame your finished prints and decorate your bedroom wall with them, or use them to make cards, bookmarks, party invitations, or anything you think of.

Sun Portraits

Calling all Picassos! See what happens when you use the sun to draw a self-portrait.

What You'll Need:
Large piece of paper, rocks, friend, markers, paint, leaves, sticks, seeds, glue

Sun's up! On a sunny morning, place a large piece of paper on the ground and put some rocks on the corners of it to keep it from blowing away. Stand next to the paper so your shadow falls on it. Then have your friend trace the outline of your shadow onto the page. You can do the same for your friend.

Now you're ready to get a little creative with your shadowy self. Using paint or markers, color your shadow or make crazy designs inside of it. If you like, make a collage inside your shadow using leaves, seeds, sticks, or whatever else you find around the yard. Come back to your creation later in the day and trace another shadow next to the one you traced earlier. Since the sun is in a different place in the sky, your shadow will have a whole new look.

The Sky's the Limit

Let your mind fly high.

What You'll Need:
Imagination, a grassy space with a view of the sky, friends (optional)

Have you ever dreamed you could fly? Here's your chance to dream with your eyes wide open. On a clear day when you can look deep into the sky, lay back in your yard or in a nearby park and let your imagination soar. Where would you fly if you could? How high would you go, if the limits were all in your mind? What would it look like and feel like up in the air? Who would you want to fly with you, if it could be anyone in the world? Try this fun fantasy on your own or get a group of friends together and share your stories.

Test Suntan Lotion

How well does your favorite lotion protect against sunrays?

What You'll Need:
Stiff cardboard,
safe scissors,
light-sensitive paper
(such as Sunprint
brand paper),
plastic wrap,
tape,
various suncreens
and tanning lotions,
keys or other
flat objects,
paper clips,
flat pan

Sunscreen and tanning lotions screen out radiation. It's the UV (ultraviolet) waves in sunlight—not the sun's heat—that browns skin and can cause sunburn or skin cancer. Many people use sunscreen to prevent UV damage. To test sunscreen and tanning lotions, make testing frames from cardboard and plastic wrap. Cut a square of cardboard four inches wider and longer than the light-sensitive paper sheets. Cut a hole in the center of the cardboard the same size as the light-sensitive paper. Cover the hole with plastic wrap and tape in place. Cut a second square of cardboard the same size as the first to go under the frame. Make as many testing frames as you need to test the various brands of lotion you have.

Put a dab of sunscreen on the plastic wrap of one frame. Spread it thinly and evenly over the entire surface. Lay a sheet of light-sensitive paper in the middle of the solid cardboard square. Set a key or similar flat object in the middle of the paper, and cover with the testing frame. Paper clip the frame to the cardboard to hold everything together.

Set the stack in bright sunlight for exactly three minutes. Bring indoors. Remove the paper and soak it in a flat pan filled with water for exactly one minute. Let the paper dry completely. Repeat the process with a clean frame for each lotion. Do one test using just the frame and no lotion at all for comparison. Which lotion worked best? Remember, the darker the paper, the more sunlight came through.

Moon Models

Learn what causes moon phases.

What You'll Need:
Two friends,
flashlight,
softball or
similar-sized ball

MANY PEOPLE think that the moon's phases are caused by the shadow of the earth moving across the face of the moon, but that isn't true. When the earth's shadow blots out the moon, we call this a lunar eclipse. To find out what *really* causes moon phases, do this simple demonstration with two friends. One person, holding a flashlight and standing near a garage in the dark is the sun. A second person, standing a few feet away, is the earth. The third person, the moon, carries a softball "in orbit" around the earth.

Have the "moon" stand directly between the "earth" and the "sun." The "earth" should see the unlit side of the moon. This is what happens when we see a new moon. We're seeing the "night side" of the moon.

Now ask the "moon" to move left of the "earth." Now the earth should see the sun side of the softball lit up and the other side in shadow. This represents a "first quarter" moon, which is really a half-moon.

Next, the "moon" stands in back of the "earth." There should be enough light reaching the softball to light up the whole side that faces the "earth." This represents a full moon.

Finally, the "moon" moves to the right of the "earth." Again, the "earth" should see half the ball lit up and half in shadow. This represents the last quarter moon. Like the first quarter moon, this is really a half-moon.

Now track the moon for a month. This is easy to do when the moon is full, because it rises just after sundown, but after that, the moon rises and sets later. Do you ever see the moon in the day? Can you figure out why?

A Lasting Step

Did you know that the footprints of the astronauts who walked on the moon in the 1960s are still there? There are no winds on the moon to blow the prints away, so Neil Armstrong's "one small step for man" is still imprinted on the moon's surface!

Planetary Walk

Take a stroll through the solar system in one thousand paces!

What You'll Need:

Ball around eight inches in diameter, three pins with small round heads, two peppercorns, small walnut, an acorn, two peanuts, index cards, glue or tape, bright markers, yardstick, large park or school grounds

HAVE YOU EVER wondered how far apart the planets really are? This planetary walk will show you just how much space there is in outer space! An eight-inch ball will be the sun. Now, glue or tape the "planets" to individual index cards, and use bright markers to label them as follows: the pinheads are Mercury, Mars, and Pluto (Pluto is actually smaller than Mercury and Mars, so if you can find a very small-headed pin, use it), the peppercorns are Venus and Earth, the walnut is Jupiter, the acorn is Saturn, and the peanuts are Neptune and Uranus.

Use your own stride as a unit of measurement. With a yardstick, practice taking steps one yard long. Each step will represent 3,600,000 miles! Now set your "sun" on the edge of a large park or on the sidewalk of a long, straight street. Take ten one-yard steps from the sun and put down your Mercury card. Does this seem a long way away? Proportionally it's in the right place. Mercury is about 36,000,000 miles from the sun.

Take nine more steps and set down Venus. Take seven steps and put down Earth. Now take 14 steps and put down Mars. You've already taken 40 steps from the sun. Earth and Mars look lonely so far from the sun and the other planets. Yet this is how they are in space. From Mars, take 95 paces and set down Jupiter. From Jupiter it's 112 steps to Saturn. 249 more paces take you to Uranus. You are halfway across the solar system!

Next is Neptune, which is 281 paces from Uranus. From Neptune, take 242 paces, and put down your last card, Pluto. You've gone 1,019 paces, or just over a half a mile. The sun probably looks like a speck, if you can see it at all. If you were standing on Pluto's surface, the sun would look about as bright as the other stars around it. Pluto is, on the average, 3,660,000,000 miles from the sun!

Night Colors

See the light show that nature puts on every evening.

What You'll Need:
Notepad and pencil,
watercolors or
colored pencils,
watch

YOU'VE PROBABLY seen a few spectacular sunrises and sunsets, but have you ever watched the whole sky to see how the colors change as the sun goes down?

On a clear evening, find a place to sit where you can watch the eastern and western horizons. Use watercolors or colored pencils to record the night sky one hour before sunset. What you should see in the east is white light near the horizon, pale blue just above it, and blue in the bowl of the sky. The western sky will look warmer than the eastern sky.

Twenty minutes before sunset, you may see pale orange at the eastern horizon, white above that, and shades of blue above that. The western sky will be full of yellows, oranges, and pinks. As the sun sets, look east to see dark blue at the horizon, brilliant shades of red, orange, or purple at the level of the setting sun's rays, and pale yellow and deep blue high above. The western sky should glow orange. If you look carefully, you might see a rare flash of green light just as the sun disappears below the horizon.

Just after sunset, the western horizon will be bright and warm with pink bands fading into purple. In the east, you'll see dark blue at the horizon, purple above that, and red in the bowl of the sky.

Twenty minutes after sunset, the western horizon may still be yellow or orange, but above is a band of rosy pink fading into purple. The eastern horizon is turning dark purple, with blue above that and purple or red in the bowl of the sky.

If there is a lot of smoke or dust in the air, the colors may be different. Heavy pollution can produce spectacular orange and red sunsets.

Kites for Kids

Fly a paper friend.

What You'll Need:
Colored paper, tape, dowel rods or wooden shish kebab sticks, safe scissors, plastic ribbon, hole punch, string

Finally, a kite you can make on your own—a kite that will actually fly! First, take an ordinary piece of 8 x 11-inch brightly colored (or brightly decorated) typing paper and fold it in half. Then fold it again along the diagonal. Fold back one side to form the kite shape. Tape along the folds. Then tape dowel rods or wood shish kebab sticks in a "x" shape on the back of the kite to give it support.

Cut six feet of plastic ribbon and tape it to the bottom of the kite. Then flip the kite over onto its back and fold the front flap back and forth so it stands straight up. Punch a hole in the flap, about a third of the way down from the top. Then tie the string to the hole, get out there, and FLY!

Cloudy Caper

Look to the sky for imaginary fun.

What You'll Need:
Cloudy day, imagination

Lots of kids have never taken the time to sit and stare at the clouds in the sky. If you're one of those kids, it's time you settled back for a fluffy white look. Lay on your back in an open field and look up at the sky. What do you see? Ordinary clouds? Or clouds shaped like your favorite cartoon or mythical beast? Do you see a cloud shaped like a fire truck or a circus tent? You never know what's going to shape up until you try.

Paper Plane Playoff

Fly high for the prize.

What You'll Need:
Paper,
paper clips,
long play area (park
or playground),
leaves (optional)

Most of us love building paper airplanes. Most of us have our own favorite designs. So why not go head-to-head with your friends' paper airplanes? Build your best paper plane. Stand side to side with your best friend and his or her plane. Now let 'em rip! After that, make the exact same alteration to each plane (add a paper clip to the nose of the plane, tear a tiny notch in the tail, or even add a small leaf to each wing). Now fly the planes again. Repeat the process until one plane is disabled. The plane that endures the most changes wins.

High-Flying Hello

Make friends with a stranger.

What You'll Need:
Helium balloons,
string,
postcard,
stamp,
pencil or pen

Buy inexpensive helium balloons, tie them together, and attach a simple "hello" postcard onto the string. Be sure to address the postcard to yourself in care of an address your folks agree is safe—like your father's work address, for example.

Add a stamp and request on the postcard that the person who finds the postcard write something and drop it in the mail. Now set the balloons free and hope for the chance to say hello to a new friend! You may be hearing from someone many miles away before you know it!

Collect Meteorites

It's easy to collect particles from outer space.

What You'll Need:
Bed sheet,
magnet,
plastic bottle

THE EARTH IS constantly bombarded with rocks from space. Most of them burn up in the atmosphere long before they touch the earth. Of the few that do drop to earth, the vast majority are as fine as dust. Tiny stone meteorites are hard to find without a microscope, but iron meteorites are easy to collect. All you need is a magnet and a bed sheet. On a still, clear night, lay a sheet on the ground. (Make sure it's in the open, away from trees.) Hold the edges of the sheet down with rocks or bricks and leave it there all night. In the morning, examine the sheet. You'll notice it's a little bit dirty. Most of this dirt is dust from the air, but some of it came from space! Take a magnet and pass it slowly over the sheet. If there are any iron particles from meteorites, they will stick to the magnet. Gently scrape the iron particles off and store them in a container, such as a plastic bottle or a film canister. Meteorite particles make a great addition to your rock collection!

Bubble Bonanza

Float some fun!

What You'll Need:
Bubble solution,
a few friends
(optional)

THERE'S NOTHING more fun than blowing hundreds and hundreds of beautiful soap bubbles. The next time you're bored and need something great to do with a breeze and a smile, why not dig out a bottle of bubbles and float on the fun? See how many bubbles you can blow, alone or with friends. See how many bubbles you can pop. See how big you can blow your bubbles or how far yours can travel before bursting. Is there a way to make bubbles extra small?

Testing the Air

How clean is the air around your home?

What You'll Need:
Stiff cardboard,
safe scissors,
hole puncher,
string,
petroleum jelly,
magnifying glass,
rubber bands

With two simple tests, you can check the air for common pollutants. In the first test, measure how much dust, dirt, soot, and other floating material is in the air. To do this, cut two pieces of stiff cardboard into a four-inch square. Punch a hole on one corner of one piece and put a string through it for hanging. Coat both sides with petroleum jelly and hang the cardboard up under the eaves of your house. Coat one side of the second piece and lay it flat in the shade, also sheltered under the eaves of your house. Leave both pieces in place for a day. Examine both cardboard squares with a magnifying glass and see if you can count the number of small particles sticking to them. Which has more particles: the cardboard that was lying flat or the one hanging?

To test for invisible gaseous pollutants, stretch three or four rubber bands over a piece of cardboard. Lay them in a shady place. Check the rubber bands each day. The faster they become brittle, the more pollutants there are in the air.

Try both of these tests in two very different places to compare pollutant levels. You might try them in the middle of a city, then in a forest or in the country.

Save our Breath

Want to help keep the air clean? Ask your parents not to idle their cars for long periods of time at a drive-through bank, dry cleaner, or restaurant. Ask them to turn their motors off while they wait, even if it's only for a few minutes. Every minute is important.

Brew Some Sun Tea

 **142**

Use solar energy to make easy and delicious iced tea.

What You'll Need:
One-quart glass jar with lid, three teabags (herb teas are recommended), liquid measuring cup, water, ice cubes, sugar and lemon (optional)

On a hot, sunny day, wash a jar in soapy water and rinse it clean. Drop in three bags of your favorite tea. (Citrus-flavored herb teas are particularly good for this.) Pour in three cups of cold water. Seal the jar and put it outside for two or three hours, keeping it in the hot sun continuously. Bring the jar indoors and remove the teabags. Put a few ice cubes in a glass and pour in the tea. Add sugar and lemon, if desired, and enjoy your tea! Leftover tea should be stored in the refrigerator. Try this with different teas. Which kind do you like best?

Starry, Starry Night

 **143**

Twinkle, twinkle, I take notes.

What You'll Need:
Notebook, pencil or pen

Are all stars the same color and brightness? Not at all. Each has dozens of distinctive qualities and characteristics based on age, distance, and light pollution. Take the time to study the starry night and make note of the different colors you see. See if you can find out why some stars seem bigger, brighter, or more colorful than others. Then hit the library or your family encyclopedia to find out if all the lights in the sky are actually stars at all.

Explore the Moon

"Travel" to the moon with binoculars and "explore" its features.

What You'll Need:
Binoculars,
paper and pencil

CHOOSE A CLEAR night with a full or nearly full moon. (The moon will rise shortly after sunset.) Sit comfortably outdoors in a place where you can see the moon. Use binoculars to look closely. What features to do you see? How many large craters do you see? Can you count the small craters? You should be able to spot Tycho crater near the southern pole and Copernicus crater near the equator and slightly west of center. Both of these craters have long, radiating, extending lines that you should be able to see through your binoculars.

These rays were caused by material flung out when the crater was created by a meteor impact. Look for the flat plains called "seas" (which don't hold water). These may have been created years and years ago when huge meteorites struck the moon and blew away huge basins that soon filled with liquid lava. The three most visible seas (or maria, as they are often called) are the Sea of Showers near the northern pole, the Sea of Serenity near the equator and to the east, and the Sea of Tranquility, just south of the Sea of Serenity.

Now draw your own moon map. Start with a large circle, then fill in all the craters and seas that you observe. Label the larger features. You can use other reference books to find names for the smaller features. If you prefer, pretend that you are the first person to explore the moon and name the features yourself!

Latitude, Altitude, Time

Measure your latitude by the north star.

What You'll Need:
Protractor,
string,
key

Long BEFORE our modern navigation systems were developed, people in ancient times navigated by the stars. The ancient Greeks, in fact, knew that the world was round and invented a system we still use to map and measure the globe. They divided the globe into latitude lines based upon the apparent altitude of the north star above the horizon.

To find your own latitude, go outdoors on a clear night and look for the north star. Tie a key or other weight to one end of a piece of string and the other end to the cross bar of a protractor. Turn the protractor so that the curved edge faces downward. Tilt it so that the string hangs exactly at "zero." Slowly tilt the protractor and look along the straight edge until you can see the north star. Notice which degree mark the string now crosses. This indicates how many degrees above the horizon the north star is. This figure is also your degree of latitude.

You can measure the altitude above the horizon of any star using the same technique, but latitude lines are based only on the angle of the north star. Try to estimate a star's altitude above the horizon with your fingers. If you hold your hand out at arm's length, the width of one finger is approximately four degrees. Your hand minus the thumb (four finger widths) is usually 15 to 16 degrees. All hands and arms are not alike, however, so check this measurement with the protractor.

Watching for Planets

Can you find the planets in the night sky?

What You'll Need:
Binoculars or telescope if desired, star chart

OF THE NINE planets in our solar system, five (besides Earth) can be seen with the naked eye. People in ancient times called the planets "wandering stars" because these bright objects appeared to change position while other stars seemed to stay in place. Try to spot the wandering stars yourself. You need only your eyes, but a pair of binoculars or a telescope offers a better look. Venus is the easiest planet to find. Look in the western sky just after the sun goes down. You can also spot it in the early morning sky just before sunrise.

The rest of the planets are harder to find. Consult an almanac or planetary table to track their movements. Watch your local newspaper or an astronomy magazine for information on which planets are visible. Use a star chart to locate the constellation where the planet will be. The planets appear to move through the constellations associated with the zodiac, so become familiar with these constellations. Once you spot a bright object that doesn't seem to belong to the constellation, try observing it through binoculars or a telescope. With most home telescopes, you can see the red spot on Jupiter and the rings of Saturn.

Sunrise, Sunset

Find out how the sun wanders with the seasons.

What You'll Need:
Sketch pad,
colored pencils

Find a place to sit where you can clearly see the eastern horizon. Sketch the horizon itself. Include any landmarks you see, such as buildings, hills, or trees. Next, find a place where you can see the western horizon and sketch that. On the first clear day of the month, go out at dawn to the spot where you sketched the eastern horizon. Watch where the sun rises and draw that in different colored pencil on one of your eastern horizon drawings. At sunset, mark the position of the sun on a drawing of the western horizon.

Try this again on the first clear day of the next month. Mark the position of the sun on the same drawings. Has its position changed? You'll probably notice that it has. If you do this once in the winter and once in the summer, you'll see a big difference! If you're patient, try marking the position of the sun once a month for a year. Why does the sun seem to move? The direction of the tilt of the earth changes in relation to the sun as the earth moves around the sun. The changing angle makes the sun appear at dawn in changing positions on the horizon.

Hot as Sun

Humans may have landed on the moon already, but you can bet they'll never set foot on the sun. The sun, which is 93 million miles away from the earth, has a temperature of about 15 million degrees Celsius. Ouch!

Let's Watch Animals

Animals come in all sizes, from giant whales to tiny mice. Insects, worms, spiders, and other creepy-crawlies are animals, too. The activities in this chapter will focus mostly on the group of animals we call *mammals*. Remember that wild mammals are very shy and come out mostly at dawn or dusk. If you want to see them in the wild, you must be quiet and very, very patient! If you're not that patient, you can watch mammals in the zoo or learn from your own pets.

On the Right Track

Bring a wild animal's foot home with you.
Well, at least in the form of a footprint!

What You'll Need:
Footprint,
narrow strip of
cardboard,
water,
pail,
plaster of paris,
stick

LEFT, RIGHT, left, right.... Your first task is to search out a well-made footprint in your yard or local park. Of course, if you see a print that resembles Big Foot's, forget what you're doing and make a beeline back to your house!

Once you have a critter's footprint in sight, press the cardboard strip into the ground to form a circular wall around the track. Now pour some water into the pail and add plaster of paris. Stir this mixture with a stick until smooth. Then pour it into the cardboard circle until it's about one inch thick. Leave the plaster to dry for about an hour.

Once the plaster is dry, carefully lift up the cardboard with the cast inside. Now remove the cardboard and—voila!—you have an animal footprint that's yours to keep!

Camouflage

Watch wild animals by using their own tricks of disguise.

What You'll Need:
Dull-colored clothing, dark green or tan tarpaulin (or blanket)

IF YOU'VE EVER walked through the woods hoping to see wild animals, you've probably been disappointed. Animals hide when they hear or smell visitors. Learn some animal hiding tricks.

BLENDING IN: Birds see in colors, so colorful clothes will give you away. Wear gray, tan, or brown. Mammals don't see color, but can tell if your clothing is light or dark compared to the background. Choose clothing that won't contrast with the background.

CHANGING SHAPE: Wild animals recognize predators and prey by their shape. Many animals have patterned coats, which make it harder for predators to spot them. Drape yourself in a dull-colored tarp or blanket and assume an outline that animals won't recognize.

UNDERCOVER: Animals hide from predators by using cover, such as bushes, trees, and rocks. Make your own cover: Drape a blanket or tarp over a low branch, tent-style, and sit under it. Be still for at least 20 minutes.

NO SCENTS: Wild mammals have an excellent sense of smell. If mammals smell you, they will stay away—even if you hide. When you choose a place to sit, make sure it is upwind of the area you're watching.

PATIENCE: Predators may hide by a water hole for hours waiting for their prey. You must be just as patient. The outdoors isn't a zoo, and animals aren't easy to find. Wild animals follow their own schedules. If you don't see any animals one day, try another day or a different area.

Can't Hide in a Cloud
Ever think you'd like to hide in a fluffy white cloud? Don't be fooled. Clouds can't hold your weight. Clouds are actually made of millions of tiny, cold water droplets, as well as some crystals of ice. So they'd be a pretty icky place to hide!

Soil Wildlife

Discover a community of creatures living under the soil!

What You'll Need:
Trowel,
shallow dish,
magnifying glass,
notebook,
pencil or pen

GO OUTDOORS with a trowel and dig around under large shrubs where leaves have fallen. Brush aside the top layer and dig up some of the partially decayed leaves and the soil underneath them. Spread your sample out in a shallow dish and observe it with a magnifying glass. Record and draw the organisms you see, such as:

EARTHWORMS: Easy to recognize by their segmented bodies.

BEETLES: These insects have six legs and a hard, shiny look. They may be black, metallic green, gold, or blue.

GRUBS: These larvae of beetles and flies are worm-like, but thick-bodied with many stumpy legs.

SPRINGTAILS: These tiny, pale, wingless insects, usually white or pale gray, have a special structure on their abdomens which they use to spring high into the air.

SPIDERS: Unlike insects, spiders have eight legs. Not all spiders weave webs. Some live and hunt near the ground.

MITES: These have eight legs, like spiders, but are round-bodied.

CENTIPEDES: Centipedes have one pair of legs per segment. They can bite, since they are predators.

MILLIPEDES: They resemble centipedes, but their legs are shorter, and they have two pairs of legs per segment. Millipedes do not bite.

Beetles, earthworms, springtails, and millipedes feed on dead plant material. By breaking leaves into tiny pieces, they make it easy for bacteria and fungi to complete the decay process. Centipedes and spiders are predators.

Backyard Wildlife Sanctuary

Make a home for wildlife in your backyard!

What You'll Need:
Gardening tools (rake, shovel, etc.), materials from the suggestions at right

OUR SUBURBAN HOMES cover a lot of land. You can give some of it back to the animals by turning your backyard into a mini-sanctuary and providing the basics: food, water, and shelter.

If you can, plant native plants that bear the fruit, nuts, seeds, nectar, and pollen that wild animals like to eat. Hazelnut trees, elderberries, service berries, huckleberries, and wildflowers are terrific.

You can also buy or build bird feeders. Fill the feeders with seeds song-birds prefer, such as sunflower seeds, white millet, and thistle. In the summer, fill hummingbird feeders with nectar made from one cup sugar and four cups water. In the winter, hang suet feeders.

Water is often scarce. One way to supply water is to set out birdbaths and keep them clean. Put the bowl of a birdbath on the ground for small mammals and ground-feeding birds. Give butterflies a drink, too. Fill a basin with sand and keep it wet. Place the basin near flowers, where butterflies visit.

Your Own Refuge!
Register your own backyard refuge with the National Wildlife Federation. To learn how, write: Backyard Wildlife Habitat Program, National Wildlife Federation, 8925 Leesburg Pike, Vienna, VA 22184-0001, or click on http://www.nwf.org.

Birds and small mammals need safe places to hide, build nests, and stay warm and dry in bad weather. If you can, plant a long hedgerow of native shrubs. Build piles of rocks, brush, or logs for small animals.

For more information on backyard wildlife sanctuaries, call your local Fish and Wildlife Department. They will have brochures and printed material to help you plan a sanctuary for your area.

Poochy Parade

Proudly parade your puppies!

What You'll Need:
Friends with dogs and leashes, accessories, portable tape or CD player

EVERYONE LOVES a parade. Everyone loves dogs. Why not combine two all-American favorites on the next sunny Saturday afternoon? Gather together all your friends with dogs and plot out the event. Whose dogs get along with other dogs? Whose dogs are better on their own? Which dogs are big? Which dogs are extra-small? Pick a theme like "Puppy Love" or "Man's Best Friend" and invent silly, inexpensive doggie accessories—red construction paper hearts gently taped to fur, poster boards hanging from the necks of each puppy's pet person. Then march to one of your favorite doggone songs—"(You Ain't Nothing But a) Hound Dog," "How Much is that Doggie in the Window?," or maybe even music from *101 Dalmatians.* Be sure someone's parent is on hand to take plenty of pictures. This will be a dog day afternoon to remember.

Feed Your Corny Friends

Make friends with bushy-tailed squirrels, one kernel at a time.

What You'll Need:
Dried corn on the cob (from animal feed or gardening stores), sturdy string, tree branches, stepping stool

IT'S NOT GOOD to feed wild animals *your* favorite foods. Sugary choices like cookies or candy can rot the teeth of wild creatures. And that's bad, because they rely on those teeth for the rest of their lives. For squirrels, nuts are an obvious alternative to candy or cookies. But so is another of our favorite foods—good old-fashioned corn. Squirrels LOVE corn, and most feed and gardening stores keep dried corn cobs in stock just for those furry friends. So why not try it yourself? Buy a bag of corn and securely tie it to the lower branches of a tree. Now sit back and watch these cute climbing rodents feast on the fun. You'll be glad you gave them real eats instead of treats.

City Wildlife Safari

There's wildlife even in the busiest parts of the city!

What You'll Need:
notepad,
pencil or pen

WHEN WE THINK of wildlife, we think of bears, cougars, bison, and other large animals. But any animal that normally lives without the care of people can be considered wildlife. This includes birds, insects, fish, and other small animals. You can find wildlife anywhere—even in a city—if you know how and where to look.

Start in a park. Sit under a group of trees and look up in the branches. Watch for birds moving around in the trees. You may also see squirrels in the branches or running around on the ground as they hunt for food. Where there are squirrels, there may also be predators, such as hawks, falcons, or foxes. Look closely at the grass, the leaves of the trees and shrubs, and in the crevices of tree bark. You're likely to find insects, spiders, and other small animals.

After the park, try watching a patch of sidewalk next to a wall or a building. It's "just" concrete, but look closer. Ants may have made a nest in a crack in the concrete. Other insects may use a wall to warm up. Birds come to hunt the insects. You may also see bats hunting insects. Don't be frightened of bats—"nature's mosquito control" aren't interested in harming you.

Keeping Warm

How do animals stay warm in the winter?
Try this experiment to find out.

What You'll Need:

Glass jars of equal size, water, thermometers, various natural insulating materials, such as leaves, soil, and dry grass, graph paper, pencil

MAMMALS HAVE fur and birds have feathers to keep them warm, but even fur and feathers aren't enough protection against stormy winter nights. How can animals keep warm enough to survive?

To find out, fill several glass jars with warm water. Record the air temperature, then put a thermometer in each jar and record the water temperature. Now insulate each jar with natural materials. Pile dry leaves around one jar and dry grass around another. Mound soil around a third. Leave one jar uninsulated for comparison.

Record the temperature of the water in each jar every five minutes until the jars all reach air temperature. Make a line graph to show how quickly the temperature fell in each jar. Which materials insulate the best? If you were an animal living in the wild, which material would you make a nest from?

Be a Squirrel

Dig This Activity!

What You'll Need:

Peanuts still in the shell, garden gloves

EVER WONDER how you'd do if you became a squirrel? Here's a way to find out. Take 30 peanuts and bury them in piles of leaves, small mounds of dirt, near trees, or in sidewalk crevices. Then, wait a week, put on your garden gloves, and try to find the peanuts you buried. Other squirrels may have gotten to your stash first—how good were your hiding places?

Sidewalk Pet Portraits

Portraits on the sidewalk.

What You'll Need:
Sidewalk,
sidewalk chalk,
neighborhood pets

DOES YOUR NEIGHBORHOOD have the world's greatest pets? Why not tell the world? Take out your sidewalk chalk and let your drawings tell the story. That big spider down the street is scary but sweet—chalk up each of his eight legs. Great Danes aren't called "great" for nothing. Draw it extra large. What's the prettiest song-bird in your tree? Let your drawings tell the story. Then sit back and watch the neighbors smile.

Water Watch

Make sure your outdoor friends never run out of water.

What You'll Need:
Old buckets,
pie pans, or
bowls,
water

THERE ARE THREE things our favorite animals need to survive—shelter, food, and water. We can't always provide shelter; moms and dads don't always feel good about inviting sparrows inside for a good night's sleep. Food can be iffy. Water, though, is a universal need, and it's one thing animals need that we can almost always supply. Set out old bowls or pie pans of water wherever you think an animal might want to drink. Then make sure they are full—check them every day. Your creature pals will thank you every time they wet their whistles.

Horsing Around

Walk, trot, or gallop your way to equestrian fun.

What You'll Need:
Friends,
long sticks,
Styrofoam chunks,
magic markers

Anyone who's ever watched a horse knows they have at least three very distinctive gaits. They walk—the same smooth motion we use when we walk. They trot—a quick step in jerky, one-at-a-time rhythm. And they gallop or canter—a smooth, graceful, long-stepped run. Why not try a game of horse follow-the-leader?

Find a stick that stands up to your belly button. This will be the body of your horse. Then, take large chunks of Styrofoam and decorate them with eyes, mouths, and a nose. This will be your horse's head. Attach the head to the stick. Hop on that horse (staying on your feet, of course) and ride! See how it feels to ride a stallion (boy horse) or a mare (girl horse).

Kitty Corner

Give your outdoor cats a warm place to curl up.

What You'll Need:
Old blankets,
newspaper
"stuffing,"
safe scissors,
needle and thread

Many cats prefer spending time outdoors. If you have a kitty friend that lives for wide-open spaces, why not cozy up a corner for those sleepier times? Does your cat have a favorite spot under the rose bush? Does she sleep on the back porch in the sun? Make a mental note of where your cat snoozes. Now, ask your parents for old newspapers, an old blanket, and a needle and thread. Cut two pieces of the blanket into heart shapes about three feet across and three feet tall. Stitch one side of the heart together at the edges to make a pillow, stuff it with newspapers, then sew up the remaining half at the edges. Then, put your cat's new special pillow in its favorite spot!

Pond Dipping

Discover the complex world of pond life.

What You'll Need:
Stiff wire coathanger, broomstick, heavy wood staples (the kind that are hammered in), tape measure, waterproof tape, safe scissors, cheesecloth or wide-mesh nylon net, needle and thread, tall rubber boots, large metal pan (such as an aluminum roasting pan), bucket

ONE WAY TO explore pond life is to make a dip net and catch living organisms for observation. To make a dip net, bend a stiff wire coat-hanger in the shape of a D, leaving the hook in the middle of the straight part of the D. Straighten the hook and use heavy wood staples to fasten the straightened hook to the end of a broomstick. Fold the wire back over the last staple. Wrap the end in waterproof tape.

Measure the distance around the wire frame. Cut some cheesecloth that width and 18 inches long. Sew the ends together into a tube. Stitch one end of the tube shut. Sew the open end of the tube to the frame by turning the edge over the frame then stitching the fabric to itself.

To use your dip net, put on rubber boots and wade into a pond (with an adult along). Be careful not to wade in water deeper than your boots. Hold the net in the water with the handle upright and the net resting on the pond bottom. Have a bucket with a little water in it ready in the other hand. Move slowly through the water and gently move the net up and down. Stop now and then and dump the contents of your net into the bucket. After you've done several nettings, come ashore and dump the bucket into a wide pan. Add a little water so your animals can swim.

When you are done, return the animals to the pond. Some pond animals (like our native turtles) are endangered because of over-collection.

Eggs Underwater

Have a close look at eggs that pond animals lay.

What You'll Need:
Shallow pan,
water,
magnifying glass

In THE SPRING, hunt around the edges of ponds in your area to look for the jelly-like eggs of frogs, salamanders, and toads. Salamander eggs lie in stiff masses, often with green algae living inside the jelly. Frog and toad eggs may be laid in strings or soft masses. Pull some loose leaves out of the water; you may find small blobs containing snail eggs on the undersides of submerged leaves. If you have an aquarium with snails, look for their eggs too.

When you find eggs, put them in a shallow pan with some water and have a look. Use your magnifying glass to observe them. Freshly laid eggs will have little for you to see, but older eggs will have tiny tadpoles inside them. Snail eggs will have tiny white embryonic snails moving slowly inside. Put the eggs back in the water and mark the spot where you found them.

Return once a week and check the progress of the eggs. See how long it takes for the tadpoles or baby snails to hatch. Don't take the eggs home in a jar to watch. It's best to leave the eggs in their natural setting, where they will be at the correct temperature and will get plenty of oxygen. The eggs will suffocate in a confined jar.

Singin' Sand

The next time you head to the beach to gather eggs, you might hear the sand sing. Some sand grains are covered with a gel. When the wind blows the grains around, they slide against each other. The gel causes the sand to make noises that sound like singing. La, la, la!

Snake Locomotion

How do snakes move without legs? Find out in this activity.

What You'll Need:

Snake (a pet or a garter snake from your backyard), sandbox or large tray filled with sand, rake

SNAKES ARE HIGHLY evolved reptiles. They move quickly without legs, which gives them some advantage over reptiles that push themselves along with legs while dragging their bellies on the ground. But how is it possible to move without legs? First, get permission to use a snake. You may have a friend who keeps a snake, or you might be able to catch a small garter snake in your backyard. If you aren't experienced in handling snakes, *get an adult to help you.*

Rake a sand box (or a sand tray) level. Use the back of a rake to make the surface smooth. Set the snake at one end of the sand and let it crawl to the other end. Put the snake safely back in its cage, then examine the tracks it left. You'll notice curved indentations in the sand where the snake's body pressed down. The snake uses the curves and coils of 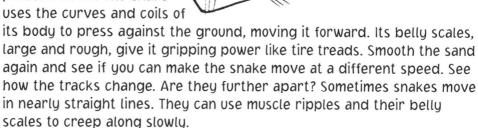 its body to press against the ground, moving it forward. Its belly scales, large and rough, give it gripping power like tire treads. Smooth the sand again and see if you can make the snake move at a different speed. See how the tracks change. Are they further apart? Sometimes snakes move in nearly straight lines. They can use muscle ripples and their belly scales to creep along slowly.

Marsh Watch

Get close to water wildlife.

What You'll Need:
Notepad and pencil

ETLANDS—freshwater marshes, salty estuaries, cold bogs, and woody swamps—are important to wildlife. Wetlands, which provide water, dense cover, and sources of food, are ideal places to watch wildlife. Look around your community for marshes and other wetlands where you can observe animals. Many wetlands are preserved in National Wildlife Refuges, in parks, and on private land. There is bound to be a place with open, shallow water that you can visit.

When you visit a marsh, move slowly and quietly so you don't disturb the wildlife, especially in the spring and early summer when birds are nesting. Find a place near the water's edge where you can sit comfortably. A good observation spot will have some shrubs you can hide under, yet still have a clear view. Be still and silent for at least 15 minutes. It takes that long or longer for the animals nearby to get used to your presence. As the animals come out and become active again, take notes on what you observe. The more often you visit, the more you will see.

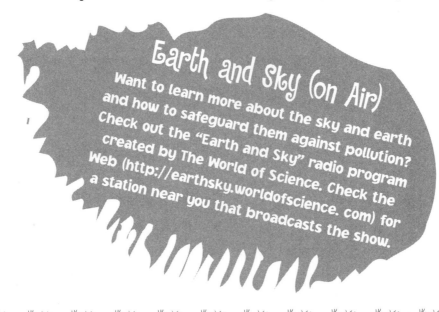

Earth and Sky (on Air)

Want to learn more about the sky and earth and how to safeguard them against pollution? Check out the "Earth and Sky" radio program created by The World of Science. Check the Web (http://earthsky.worldofscience.com) for a station near you that broadcasts the show.

Trail Tales

Find some animal tracks and try to figure out what the animal was doing.

What You'll Need:
Garden gloves,
a forest, meadow,
or beach

OBSERVING ANIMAL TRACKS is like reading a detective story. Tracks give us clues about what animals do. Look for animal tracks in freshly fallen snow, on sandy beaches, or in the mud along streams and ponds. Tracks are easier to see if you walk toward the sun, because the shadows make them more distinct.

When you find tracks, stop and have a close look. (Push away any leaves and rocks in the way.) Try to determine what animals were there. You'll probably find lots of cat and dog tracks, but you may also see tracks of raccoons, rabbits, muskrats, or large birds. What was the animal doing? Did it come by the water for a drink? Was it traveling across an open field in the snow? If the tracks are deep and far apart, the animal may have been running. Are other tracks nearby? Could one animal have been following the other?

If you see many tracks in one spot, perhaps the animal was nosing around looking for something to eat. Try to follow the tracks as far as you can. If you lose the trail, mark the last track you found and move in circles around it, wider and wider, until you find the next track.

Mouse Near the House?

Learn to spot signs of small rodent activity in your neighborhood.

What You'll Need:
Powers of observation

SMALL RODENTS, such as mice and voles, are shy creatures active mostly at night. You may never know there are any around, but rodents leave behind signs that they've been active. Look around your house and yard, especially at the base of a wall.

Do you see gnawed nuts or cherry pits? Mice chew holes in cherry pits to get at the seed inside. Look also for holes near the base of the wall. These may be mouse holes. Hunt around under pine trees. Can you find pine cones that have been gnawed apart? Squirrels often feed on pine cones, and so do mice.

Look in bark dust and other loose mulch for small, raised tunnels near the surface. Voles, often called meadow mice, make these tunnels as they search for plant material. While mice eat mostly seeds, voles eat other kinds of plant material, including flower bulbs. Gardeners don't like vole tunnels in their flower beds.

Not a Small Pest

If the biggest pest around your house is a mouse, feel lucky. A 33-foot-long, tank-like armored dinosaur lived in north America more than 70 million years ago. Fossil evidence tells us that the creature even had armor plating on its eyelids.

How Tadpoles Breathe

With a steady hand and some patience,
you can watch tadpoles breathe.

What You'll Need:
Tadpole,
clear plastic cup,
pond water,
eyedropper,
food coloring

Look in shallow ponds for tadpoles. Catch one good-sized tadpole and put it in a clear plastic cup of pond water. When the tadpole is sitting still, fill an eyedropper with food coloring. Slowly and gently lower the tip of the eyedropper into the water until the tip is close to the tadpole's mouth. You may want to practice with a water-filled eyedropper until you can do this without disturbing the tadpole.

Once the eyedropper is in place, slowly squeeze out one drop of food coloring into the water in front of the tadpole. Slowly and carefully remove the eyedropper and closely observe the tadpole. If the animal hasn't moved, colored water will soon stream out from of the gills on the sides of the tadpole's head. The tadpole breathes by drawing water through its mouth and passing the oxygen-rich water across gills that contain small blood vessels. The tadpole takes in oxygen from the water and releases carbon dioxide. The water passes out of the gill openings.

Fish Respiration

Fish breathe underwater, which means they take in oxygen instead of the air that you breathe. While a fish swims through the water, its gills absorb the oxygen in the water and pass it through its bloodstream and membranes.

Our Fun, Feathered Friends

Few animals are easier to watch than birds. Maybe that's why feeding backyard birds is so popular. Songbirds are protected by federal law, yet many birds still have problems surviving because people shoot them, cats hunt them, and construction and development destroy their nesting areas. The activities in this chapter will help you learn about birds and give you ideas about how you can help them survive.

It's For the Birds

Here's the perfect bird feeder to help you get up close and personal with some hummingbirds!

What You'll Need:
Wide-mouthed container (like a margarine tub), hole puncher, four pieces of string (each measuring about a foot long), sugar, water, beet juice

Zip! If you blink, you just might miss a speedy hummingbird. But this simple feeder will keep hummers coming back for more—and you just might get a chance to spot one after all.

First, you'll need to punch four evenly spaced holes around the container, about a half-inch from the top. Thread a string through each hole and tie each one to keep it in place. Then take the loose ends of the string and tie them together. You'll use this end to hang the feeder.

Mix the sugar, water, and beet juice (the color will attract the hummingbirds) in the container. Now you're ready to hang the feeder on a tree outside. Happy hummer-watching!

# Birds of a Feather

Feather your nest, then find out whose feathers you found!

What You'll Need:
Brown paper
lunch bag,
gardening gloves
(optional),
walking stick,
spiral notebook,
tape,
markers

FINDING A FEATHER is a wonderful treat. It's like discovering a natural treasure in your own backyard. So why not go on a full-scale search? Grab a paper lunch sack, slip on your sneakers, and head outside.

Keep your eyes peeled. Remember that feathers are light and easily caught by the wind, so carefully use your gloves and walking stick to rummage through piles of natural debris blown against large stones or fallen logs. When you find your feathers, slip them into your paper bag for safekeeping until you get home.

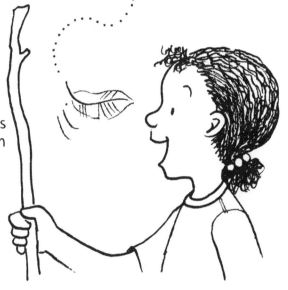

Once you do, ask your parents or adult neighbors if they can help you identify what bird lost each feather. Use library books or the Internet to find pictures of the birds. Tape the feathers inside a spiral notebook and make a few notes about what secrets each one revealed.

Be sure to wash your hands with soap and warm water whenever you handle wild feathers of any kind. Feathers can carry germs.

Watch the Birdie

Document which fine feathered friends call *your* home "home."

What You'll Need:
Bird feeders,
bird seed,
paper,
pen or pencil

Our fine feathered friends help maintain the balance of nature. When you keep a record of just what birds flutter by your window, you begin to understand how that balance works. Why not set a few minutes aside each day to keep track of which birds (and how many) call your house "home sweet home"? Use a few inexpensive bird feeders filled with seed to draw your birds near (this book has some bird feeders you can make on your own). Then sit back and enjoy the show, making sure to take notes on what you see and when you see it.

Guest in the Nest

Help indigenous birds feather their nests.

What You'll Need:
Hair from a
hairbrush,
cotton balls,
dryer lint,
bits of yarn

If spring has sprung in your hometown, it's probably time for your local birds to start laying a few eggs. But even birdie babies require a nursery. This season, you can help birds line their nests. The next time your hairbrush gets crammed full of tangled tendrils, don't just pull the hair out and throw it away. Weave it into the branches of a tree that's a known hangout for birds.

Have a few dusty cotton balls that are headed for the trash? Pull them apart and hook them onto the branches as well. Do the same with dryer lint and bits of yarn left over from a knitting spree. Before you know it, those bits and pieces will mysteriously vanish from the trees. They will reappear, mixed with mud and branches, as the birds' nests take shape.

Bird Track Tracing

Make an impression—capture the bird tracks.

What You'll Need:
Old cake pan or
cookie sheet,
soft, wet mud or
sand,
bird feeder,
bird seed,
plaster of paris,
old bowl and spoon
to mix plaster

Have you ever really looked at the delicate tracks of your neighborhood birds? This is your chance to capture and keep a little bird scratch all your own.

Pick an area near a tree often inhabited by birds. Now fill an old cake pan or cookie sheet about halfway with soft, wet mud or very fine sand. Don't fill it too high. It should be wet enough to leave a good impression when you press a dime into the surface and then take the dime away.

Fill an ordinary bird feeder with bird seed, set the seed at the end of the pan, then scram. Come back in a few hours (or the next day) and see what tracks your feathered friends have made. For extra fun, carefully fill the pan the rest of the way with plaster of paris. Once the plaster dries, you'll have a perfect raised cast of your bird track experiment.

Peep, Peep!

Could you make yourself understood using peeps and squawks?

What You'll Need:
Patience,
imagination,
a willing friend,
one free hour

As humans, we take our ability to communicate for granted. But what if you suddenly had only chirps and peeps to make your ideas understood? What if our words—hundreds and hundreds of them—were replaced with bird-like tweets and whistles? Take an hour to find out. Try to share one hour with a friend or family member without saying a single word. Chirp when you're hungry. Squawk when you don't like what you've heard. Whistle a happy song when you're content. See if words are the only sounds worth understanding. Then, go outside and try to have a conversation with the birds you see.

Experimental Parent

Sit still long enough to learn how it feels to be a bird.

What You'll Need:

Large "nest" of straw or leaves, plastic Easter eggs, companion

IF YOU'VE EVER wondered what it takes to change a clutch of eggs into baby birds, check out the idea we're hatching now. It may look easy to be a mother bird. After all, all they do is sit, right? Wrong. Experts say bird embryos undergo 42 different stages of growth inside the egg. If the mother doesn't turn and care for each egg, the chick might not survive. So why not experiment with warming a nest of your own?

Make a nest out of straw and leaves and then sit still on a few plastic eggs of your own. Keep all the eggs warm to the touch. Turn them all over at least once or twice an hour. And don't forget, you'll need a friend or pretend bird mate to bring you food and give you potty breaks if you're going to pull this experiment off. Sit for three or four hours to get an idea of how much it takes to raise a baby bird. You'll understand just how important a mother bird is to her unborn babies.

Raising Chicks

Not all birds raise their babies the same way. In some species of birds, both mothers and fathers take care of the little ones, but most birds rely more on the female to handle the rearing and the male to find food.

Bird Cafeteria

Set out a feast for the birds and learn what they like best.

What You'll Need:
Bird feeders
(purchased or
homemade),
thistle seeds,
cut-up fruit,
nail,
hammer,
dull knife,
whole coconut,
adult help, drill,
cracked corn,
suet,
peanuts,
string,
mesh bag

MANY PEOPLE put out feeders full of seeds, but you can attract a wider range of birds by offering a selection of foods. Try the following ways of offering foods and see what your birds like best:

• Offer various seeds. You can buy special feeders for fine thistle seed and for larger sunflower seeds. Offer thistle in the summer when goldfinches are around. Sunflower seeds can be out all year.

• Build or buy a table-style feeder on a post to offer peanuts and cut-up fruit (especially cherries).

• Pound a slender nail into a tree and stick half an apple on it, or wedge apple slices between tree branches.

• Cut an orange in half and hang the halves from a branch for orioles.

• Cut a coconut in half. Drill a hole near the edge and hang from a tree branch. Small, seed-eating birds like to peck at the meat, and larger, more aggressive birds cannot get to it easily.

• On a large flat rock, offer cracked corn to quail and doves.

• Use a flat window feeder to offer cut-up suet from the meat counter. Make sure the window is high enough that dogs, cats, and rats cannot reach. Don't offer suet in the warmer months; it spoils quickly.

Bake a Bird Cake

Make your feathered friends happy.

What You'll Need:
Bread crumbs,
unsalted nuts,
raisins,
sugar,
corn meal,
flour,
bird seed,
peanut butter,
bacon drippings,
string

WHEN WE CELEBRATE OUR favorite friends, we bake them a cake. We can celebrate our feathered friends the same way—by making them a special bird cake and watching them feast off it for days. Begin with two cups of bread crumbs (use mom's old, dry bread crusts—the birds won't mind, and mom will like the fact that they don't go to waste). Mix in a handful of unsalted nuts, two handfuls of raisins, one cup of sugar, a half-cup of corn meal, a half-cup of flour, and one cup of bird seed. Add eight ounces of peanut butter and some bacon drippings to hold the mix together. Shape the bird snack into "donuts" and freeze. Once they're frozen, carefully hang the bird cakes from your favorite trees and watch the birds chow down.

Milk Carton Meal

Put those old milk cartons to good use.

What You'll Need:
Empty milk carton,
bird cakes,
hole puncher,
string

IF YOUR YARD is a little short on trees with bending branches, hang your bird cakes in special milk carton feeders. Make the bird cake recipe listed above. Then, instead of shaping the mixture into donuts, fill the bottom of a milk carton with the treat. Punch holes in the carton and run strings from corner to corner, tying them together where they meet at the top. Hang these treats from rain gutters or flagpoles to provide your birds a safe and delicious treat.

Plant For Your Birdies

Grow a home for your feathered friends.

What You'll Need:
Seeds,
tree saplings,
flower starts

WHY NOT PLAN your gardens around the birds you want to attract? Studies show birds prefer these five types of plants when searching for the ideal place to nest and live. Evergreens provide cover, winter shelter, and summer nesting sites. Grass (especially if not mowed during nesting season) provides cover for ground-nesting birds. Nectar-producing plants (especially red blossoms) attract hummingbirds and orioles. Fruiting trees and bushes, like cherry trees and grapevines, attract dozens of species of birds for obvious (and tasty) reasons. Be sure to plant trees or bushes that bear fruit every season. Nut and acorn plants, such as oaks, chestnuts, walnuts, and hazelnuts, are good for birds to eat and provide good nesting sites.

Bird-Mart

Make a "home supply" stop for busy birds.

What You'll Need:
Large cardboard
box,
safe scissors,
string,
yarn,
dryer lint,
hair from combs
and brushes

WHEN NESTING time arrives, transform your yard into bird central with this cardboard bird-nest superstore! Cut holes and notches in a large, sturdy cardboard box. Now feed bits of string, yarn, dryer lint, and hair into those holes and notches. Place the box on a high table or on top of a flat roof, then wait and watch. Before you know it, dozens of backyard birds will land on your cardboard shop just to find special things for the nests they're building.

Tweet Repeat

Learning a new language is always an adventure, especially when you learn to speak bird.

What You'll Need:
Tape recorder, bird sounds

SET A TAPE RECORDER on "record" and place it near a spot where local birds perch and sing. Slip your recorder inside a paper bag (with a hole cut near the microphone) to protect it from the droppings that sometimes go along with fluttering birds. Let the tape record for at least 15 minutes. Then retrieve your recorder and carefully study the sounds as you play them back from the tape. See if you can mimic the sounds. Practice until it sounds just right. Then sing away when a bird is nearby. Do the tiny creatures react? You'll never know until you try.

Is Bigger Faster?

How do birds take off for flight?

What You'll Need:
Birds to watch, stopwatch, notebook, pencil or pen

ARE BIGGER BIRDS faster birds? Are smaller birds in more danger? Are the answers as obvious as they seem? Study your neighborhood birds to find out. Sit quietly somewhere that birds like to search for food, water, and shelter. Time exactly how long it takes each species to go from ground to treetop. Keep careful notes. You may find that while bigger birds have stronger wings, they also have more weight to launch into flight. You may find that smaller birds beat their wings faster but rise no faster than their bigger, more powerful friends. You may discover that it depends entirely on the individual bird. But whatever you observe, you're sure to find the study is a real "tweet."

Ring a Bell

Help save your neighborhood birds.

What You'll Need:
Large jingle bells,
string,
safe scissors,
ladder

DOMESTIC HOUSECATS on the prowl don't mean any harm when they instinctively hunt birds. But they *are* responsible for the decline of many American songbirds. You can help even the odds. Go to your local craft store and buy the kind of jingle bells you might use during the holiday season. With adult help, tie the bells (on strings) to the lower branches of your songbirds' favorite roost. When cats climb or jump to the lower branches, the birds will have a little extra warning—and time to escape.

Bird Do's and Don'ts

Let nature take its course.

What You'll Need:
Patience

WHEN WE SEE A baby bird fall from the nest, it's only natural to want to scoop it up and offer it protection. But when we try to help, we often cause harm. So the next time you see a helpless nestling, take these steps instead.

Try not to pick up the bird unless it is clearly wounded and in danger from another animal. Assuming the bird is not in immediate danger, don't stay too close to the bird or its mother's nest, and don't try to call the bird's mother.

Do move back at least 20 feet from the nesting site, keep quiet, and keep all cats and dogs from the area. Be patient and wait for the mother bird to take care of her hatchling in her own way.

Seed and Feed

Keep your favorite feathered friends from going hungry.

What You'll Need:
Bird seed,
stiff paper plates or
recycled pie pans,
hole puncher,
string,
safe scissors

HAVE YOU EVER noticed exactly where your favorite birds like to gather to eat? Have you ever watched to see what they eat while they're there? You can lend them a hand. Go to your local pet or garden center and buy a bag of bird seed made just for the birds in your yard. Now fill stiff paper plates or recycled pie pans with the seed and string them to lower branches of the trees to help make sure each tweeter gets enough to eat.

Cousin Dino

Find modern day dinosaurs in feathers.

What You'll Need:
Notebook paper,
pencil

MORE AND MORE dinosaur scientists (called paleontologists) believe birds could be modern dinosaurs. Do you agree? Make a few comparisons of your own to find out. How are birds and dinosaurs different? How are they alike?

Go outside and look closely at the feet of your local birds. How many claws are on their feet? What are the scales like on the skin of those feet? What kind of tracks do they leave behind as they walk? What do their eyes look like? Where are they placed on their tiny bird heads? By examining modern birds and comparing what you discover to details of extinct dinosaurs, you can decide for yourself!

Down and Out

How warm are our feathered friends?

What You'll Need:

Down jacket or comforter, regular jacket or comforter

IT'S HARD TO BELIEVE feathers keep a bird so warm even when rain falls and snow flies. You can find out how it works by wrapping yourself in down. What is down? In simple terms, down is a layer of feathers. On a bird, down is the term for its fluffy little feathers, rather than its long, spiny quills. In coats and bedspreads, down is a stuffing of small feathers, whether fluffy or not.

No matter what the definition, the way down works remains the same. Layers of natural feathers hold warmth in. So wrap up warmly in a down jacket or bedspread (ask permission before you use the bedspread) and head out into a frosty winter day. Stand in the cold for a few minutes. Now go inside and change into a regular jacket or wrap up in an ordinary cotton blanket. Spend a few moments in the same cold. Which wrap kept you warmer? Nine times out of ten, down will win.

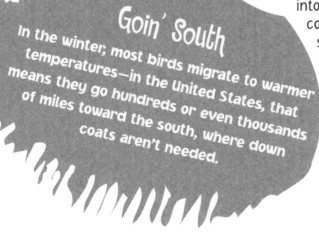

Goin' South

In the winter, most birds migrate to warmer temperatures—in the United States, that means they go hundreds or even thousands of miles toward the south, where down coats aren't needed.

Migrating Birds

Follow the spring and fall bird migrations in your area.

What You'll Need:
Binoculars,
bird manual for
your area,
notebook,
pencil or pen

IF YOU LIVE in the middle of one of the major flyways, you're in a great place to watch the annual bird migrations. Even if you're not near a flyway, you may still spot birds migrating through your area. Flyways are simply where the birds concentrate. Because many migratory birds are attracted to wetlands, locate a marsh, pond, or lake in your area. Find a place near the water where you can watch birds. Use binoculars for a better look. A good bird manual can help. Some of the most common migratory water birds you'll find all over the United States are canada geese, pintail ducks, mallard ducks, and red-winged blackbirds.

Take notes about the birds you see. You'll probably see a lot more species during the migratory season than at other times. Some birds will stay all year. Others are just passing through. Notice also which birds migrate to your area to stay a season. You may have heard that geese fly south for the winter and north for the summer. But watch what happens in your area. People in certain areas are puzzled when they see geese flying all directions in their area all winter long. They expect the geese to "fly south for the winter," but where geese end up may be as far "south" as they fly. The flocks will remain all winter before returning to their nesting grounds in Canada and Alaska.

Bird Journal

Keep track of the birds you see and learn more about them.

What You'll Need:
Composition book or notebook, pen or pencil, bird-shaped stickers or bird pictures (optional), binoculars, bird guide for your area

Most birders keep track of the birds they have seen. You can start your own bird journal and use it every time you go out looking for birds. Get a sturdy, bound notebook, preferably one with a hard cover. An ordinary composition book will work very well. If you like, decorate your notebook with bird stickers or cut-out pictures of birds. Reserve the first two or three pages for your "life list"—a listing of every kind of bird you've seen. You will add to your list each time you go outdoors and spot a new bird you haven't seen before.

Now find some good places to watch for birds. Feeding stations, parks, ponds, shores, marshes, meadows, and fences are great places. Take your journal with you each time you go. Find a comfortable spot to sit, and stay quiet as you watch for birds. Take a pair of binoculars with you if you have them. On the top of a fresh page, write down where you are, the time of day, and the date. These are important, because you won't see the same birds everywhere, and you'll see different birds each season. List the names of the birds you see. Sketch or write a description of birds you don't recognize.

Join and Bird!

The Audubon Society is an organization for people who love to watch birds. Contact your local chapter of the Audubon Society if you're interested in joining a bird-watching club, doing projects that help birds, or taking part in the annual bird census.

Note as many features of the bird as you can so you can look it up later. Record what the birds are doing. Are they feeding, flying, singing, fighting, or displaying? Is there a bird on a nest? Your bird journal entries will teach you a lot about birds. You'll be able to tell which birds migrate through your area and which stay a whole season or all year. You'll get a pretty good idea of which birds are most common, too.

Sapsuckers and Woodpeckers

Follow the clues to find out what's been in your trees!

What You'll Need:
Powers of observation

SAPSUCKERS AND woodpeckers have chisel-like beaks that they use to drill holes in trees. Both feed along tree trunks, but eat different kinds of foods. Woodpeckers eat insects, and drill for them with their beaks. Sapsuckers punch holes in trees, then lick up the sweet sap with their long tongues. Look around your yard or a park for trees with small holes in them. Notice the pattern of the holes.

Woodpeckers eat insects wherever they find them, leaving holes randomly scattered around the tree. Sapsuckers feed more systematically. They will patiently drill a straight line of holes across the tree trunk. By the time the bird finishes drilling the last hole, the first is full of sap. The bird then drinks the sap from each hole, first to last, in turn. When the holes stop dripping sap, the sapsucker drills some more. If you see horizontal rows of holes along a tree trunk, you know the sapsuckers have been at work. If you like, hide behind a bush or a tree near the tree where woodpeckers or sapsuckers have been working. If you're patient enough, the birds might return and you can watch them feed.

Be a Bird Behaviorist

190

Why do birds do what they do? Watch the birds and find the answers yourself.

What You'll Need:
Notebook and pencil,
binoculars,
bird guide for
your area

BECAUSE BIRDS ARE active in the day and aren't too shy, they make terrific subjects for studies of behavior. See how much you can learn from the birds in your area. An easy way to study birds is to set up a feeding station in your yard (see the "Bird Cafeteria" activity for suggestions) that you can see from a window.

Set up a comfortable chair in front of the window and be ready to write down what you see. At first you may only see a confusing jumble of activity, with birds flying this way and that. Some will be at a feeder one moment and on the ground the next. They never stop moving. How can you make sense of what you see?

The best way is to pick something out of the action to observe. You might first observe just one bird. Follow it with your eyes and describe what it does. Then, watch one bird feeder. Describe how the birds act when they are on the feeder. Finally, look for one kind of behavior. Count how many times one bird chases another away from food, for instance. By watching a flock of birds carefully, and noting who chases who, you may be able to determine which birds dominate the flock. You can also watch for any peculiar or interesting behavior. For instance, you may notice Downy woodpeckers work up a tree trunk as they find insects in the bark. Watch how nuthatches and brown creepers go down the tree headfirst to find insects the woodpeckers miss.

Birds Big and Small

The largest bird alive today is the ostrich. It can reach nine feet tall and lays three-pound eggs. The smallest bird is the bee hummingbird, which measures just two inches long! It lays two eggs at a time, each about the size of a human pinky nail.

Food for Flyers

Try these ideas for simple bird feeders.

What You'll Need:

Scrap wood, saw,
outdoor paint,
metal brackets,
peanut butter,
lard or shortening,
pine cones or
yogurt cups,
half-pint berry
basket,
string, safe scissors

WHETHER YOU'RE setting up a backyard wildlife refuge or just want to attract a few birds, you'll enjoy having and maintaining bird feeders in your yard. To make a window feeder, cut a piece of scrap wood (with adult help) as wide as a window. Paint it, then use metal brackets to mount it underneath a window. You can offer seeds, fruit, or cut-up suet on a table. You can also set out a shallow dish of water for the birds to drink.

Straight peanut butter is too sticky for birds, but you can mix it with equal parts lard or shortening, then stir in corn meal and sunflower seeds until the mixture is stiff. Stuff the mix into pine cones and hang them up, or spoon into yogurt cups and hang the cups in trees.

To make a fruit feeder, tie long strings to the corners of a half-pint plastic berry basket. Tie the strings together and hang the basket from a tree branch. Put a few cut cherries, grapes, or other diced, brightly-colored fruit in the basket. Offer a small amount of fruit at a time and replace the fruit daily. Offer this in the summer when fruit-eating birds are active.

On Hummingbirds

Watching a hummingbird at your feeder is tough. Not only is a hummingbird tiny, it's also very fast. A hummer can go up to 50 miles per hour! It flies so fast that you can't see its wings flap. And better yet, hummers can even fly backwards!

Eat Like a Bird

Think birds don't eat much? Think again.

What You'll Need:
Ordinary meals broken up into about two dozen tiny meals, one free day

WHEN PEOPLE SAY, "You eat like a bird," they often mean you hardly eat anything at all. But modern bird scientists (called "ornithologists") have a different perspective. They say that although birds do eat tiny mouthfuls of food, they do so hundreds and hundreds of times each day. They have to eat a lot just to keep their energetic little bodies moving.

So why not try a bird's eating habits on for size? You might not want to feast on invertebrates (bugs & worms), but you can try to eat your food gradually, one tiny bite at a time. See how it affects your energy levels. See how it affects those hunger pains you usually feel three times a day. You may never look at birds the same way again.

How Close?

Prove you can watch without wounding.

What You'll Need:
Ruler

CAN BIRDS LEARN to trust the humans in their world? Why not take a summer to find out? Watch your yard to find out where birds like to gather. First, watch them from your house, talking softly as you look. Then, move outside, but stay close to your house, again talking very softly. Move just two feet closer each day, being careful to sit still and make no sudden movements. How close can you get to your feathered friends? If you're patient, you might be surprised.

Egg-sploration

Find out what birds leave behind.

What You'll Need:
Stepladder,
adult help,
work gloves,
soap

WHEN THE NESTING season in your region is over, why not go on a little egg-sploration of your own? Go from tree to tree in an area where birds nest and step up to a whole new world of information. With adult help, use a stepladder to reach abandoned nests. Be sure to wear gloves to protect your hands from bacteria and tiny insect pests.

What do you find inside the nest? Are there tiny eggshell fragments? Whole eggs that didn't successfully hatch? What story do these eggshells tell? How do different eggshell colors differ from nest to nest? You never know what fun facts you'll hatch next. When you are finished looking at the nests, leave everything where it was. Be sure to wash your hands with antibacterial soap as soon as you finish this activity.

Stopwatch Takeoff

How long does it take a bird to reach the sky?

What You'll Need:
Stopwatch,
paper,
pencil or pen

HOW LONG does it take the average bird to go from land to air? That depends on the bird. Do your own personal study. Take your stopwatch outside to your favorite bird sanctuary. The instant you see a bird take off, hit the "start" button. Stop timing when the bird reaches clear sky. Make a note of the time you've logged and the kind of bird that set that pace. Now search for another kind of bird and repeat the process. When you compare notes, you'll be amazed by the individual start-to-finish potential of different birds.

Water Holes

Attract more wildlife to your backyard by offering water all year 'round.

What You'll Need:
Hose with nozzle, water, pie pan, pea gravel, garbage can lid, small, rigid-sided plastic wading pool, shovel, newspaper, flat river rocks

IF YOU WERE a bird, could you find enough places in your neighborhood to drink? Do your local water sources dry up or freeze? Make life easier for wildlife with a human-made oasis. First, put a fan-shaped nozzle on the end of a hose and lay the hose in a flower bed or garden that needs watering. Turn the hose on to make a slow, gentle stream. Let the water run across the garden. Birds will be attracted in the evening after a long, thirsty day.

For a pie-pan bird bath, set a large pie pan on level ground. Pour a thin layer of fine gravel into the bottom and add a rock for birds to sit on and weigh the pan down. Pour in an inch of water. To make a garbage can-lid bird bath, excavate a shallow hole in the ground and set the lid in it. Sprinkle gravel in the bottom, add some rocks, and pour in an inch of water. During the winter, have an adult help you keep the water from icing over.

Or for a plastic wading pool pond, have an adult help dig a hole six inches wider and three inches deeper than the pool. Pour three inches of pea gravel in the bottom for drainage. Put an inch-thick layer of newspapers on the gravel to cushion the pond bottom. Set the wading pool in the hole. Add flat rocks on the bottom of the pool and rocks on one side to make a shallow bathing area. Fill the pool with water. Fill in around the outside of the pool with more gravel. Place rocks, small logs, and plants around the edge to make the pond attractive to wildlife.

Inside Insects
(and Other Little Lives)

Do spiders give you the creeps? Do bugs gross you out? Do worms make you squirm? Let the activities in this chapter help you overcome your fears of these tiny beasts, some of which are among the most useful animals on earth. Where would we be if bees stopped pollinating the flowers on fruit trees and other crops? What would happen to our soil if worms suddenly disappeared? Try these activities to learn why these small animals are so important.

Hungry Ants

197

What kinds of food do our small friends like?

What You'll Need:
Ant hill, jar of honey, leaves or grass, bread crumbs, sugar, piece of lettuce, small amount of tuna fish, spoon

FIND AN ANTHILL somewhere around your house, either on a sidewalk or a patch of dirt. Make sure it's in use by looking for signs of activity. Once you've found an active anthill, plan a test to find out what different types of foods the ants enjoy eating.

Spread some honey on a couple of leaves or blades of grass, lay out some small bread crumbs, spread out a little sugar, tear up lettuce into tiny pieces, and spoon out a bit of tuna fish. Make sure the different foods are at least an inch apart and that they're an equal distance from the ant colony. Come back a few minutes after you've put the food out to see what the ants are taking and what they're leaving. What do the foods the ants take have in common? What about the foods they *don't* want?

Worm Observations

Worms are interesting if you observe them up close.

What You'll Need:

Earthworms,
trowel,
plastic container
of moist dirt,
paper towels, water,
magnifying glass,
cotton swab,
alcohol or fingernail
polish remover

CAREFULLY DIG UP some worms in a garden and put them in a container. Prepare a worm-friendly surface for your observations. Lay three thicknesses of paper towel on a waterproof surface and moisten the paper until very wet. Set the worm on the wet paper towel.

ON THE OUTSIDE: Look for a wide, thick band around the worm's middle. This is called a clitellum. It is closest to the head end. Look at the head with your magnifying glass. See if you can find the mouth, with its over-hanging lip. Notice that the worm's body is made up of segments. Each segment has two pairs of special bristles (called setae). Wet your fingers and run them down the worm's body to feel the rough setae.

GETTING AROUND: Let the worm crawl on the paper towel. When it wants to move, it becomes long and thin. If you touch it, the worm contracts and becomes thicker. The worm has two layers of muscles; those running around the body squeeze the worm and make it thinner and longer. Those running end to end make the worm shorter and thicker.

HEARTBEATS: Find a light-colored worm. Wet its upper surface and use your magnifying glass to observe the upper surface near the head. Look for the worm's five beating hearts.

STRONG REACTIONS: Dip a cotton swab in alcohol or nail polish remover. Hold the swab close to the worm's head, but DON'T touch the worm with the strong chemical. What happens when the swab is near the head? Does the worm move? Hold the swab near the tail, then near the middle. Can the worm detect where the fumes are? How does it react?

Moth Navigation

Why do moths fly into candles and lamps?

What You'll Need:
Street (with street lamp)

On a night when the moon is full, stand on a street where you can see the moon. Turn your head so that you see the moon over one shoulder. Now walk down the sidewalk and watch the moon over your shoulder. Note that you don't have to move your head as you go. The moon seems to follow you. (It doesn't *really*, of course.)

Now find a lit street lamp. Look over one shoulder at it. Walk and watch the lamp over the same shoulder. Feel like you're walking in circles? To keep the lamp over the same shoulder, you have to walk *around* it.

Moths use the moon to navigate. The moon doesn't move out of position if the moth flies in a straight line. But street lamps are confusing. If the moth flies in a straight line, it thinks the lamp's position has changed. As the moth continues, the lamp "moves" again. The moth flies in circles, moving closer and closer until it is trapped.

Mini-Sanctuary

Create homes for the smallest wildlife in your yard!

What You'll Need:
Chunk of backyard space, rocks, old clay pots, bricks, hunks of wood (the older the better), posterboard, pen

Get permission to use a sheltered corner of the yard. Don't clear away old sticks and weeds, which give shelter and food to the creatures you want to protect. Place broken clay pots upside down in the shade for snails and toads. Make a small rockpile in the sun for flying insects and small reptiles. Prop up a brick with small flat rocks for insects to inhabit. Set out old wood as homes for beetles and ants.

Many weeds serve as food for butterflies and rodents, but pull big vines like blackberries or large, aggressive shrubs that could take over the space. Once you're done, draw a sign reading, "Mini-wildlife refuge. Come and enjoy!" That way, visitors won't clean up the "mess"!

Worm Food

Have you ever tried feeding worms?

What You'll Need:
Coarse netting (such as an old onion or orange sack), small leaves, tent stakes, notebook, pencil or pen

PICK A SPOT on the lawn with thick, green grass and soft soil. Worms will be active in this area. When the lawn has been mowed and watered and the grass is short, lay out some fallen leaves. Cover the leaves with netting and use tent stakes to hold the netting in place. (This will keep the leaves from blowing away.) In your notebook, sketch the pattern of leaves exactly as you see them. Label this picture "Start."

Check the netting the next day. Have any leaves disappeared? Draw what you see, and label the picture "Day one." Continue checking the netting each day to see if more leaves disappear. Make a new drawing each day. Worms like to grab leaves and pull them down in their burrows to munch on later. You probably won't see *all* the leaves disappear, but worms active in the spot you choose will probably take away some of them.

Warm Bugs, Cold Bugs

How do insects react to changes in temperature outdoors?

What You'll Need:
Sunny flower border, outdoor thermometer, notebook, pencil

IF A sunny flower garden is in your yard or a nearby park, you can easily discover what effects temperature has on insects. Spring is a good time to do this, because the temperature can be warm one day and cold the next. On a warm day, check an outdoor thermometer to see the temperature. Take your notebook and sit near the flower border where you can see insects. Pick a patch of flowers about a yard square. Every few minutes, count how many insects fly around in the flowers. On a cold day, repeat the experiment. Watch the same flowers and count the number of flying insects. On which day were the insects most active? How could this affect the plants in the border if those insects pollinate some of the flowers?

Can Insects See Color?

Set up an experiment to test the color vision of bees.

What You'll Need:
Sugar,
water,
pan,
colored paper,
safe scissors,
clear plastic cups,
outdoor table,
heavy washers,
notebook

MAKE NECTAR to attract bees by mixing one quarter-cup of sugar with one cup of water. With help, heat the mixture slowly in a pan on the stove until the sugar dissolves. Let the mix cool.

Then, cut squares of colored paper four inches on each side. Use red, orange, yellow, green, blue, deep blue, violet, white, black, and gray. Cut the bottoms out of as many clear plastic cups as you have squares of paper. Tape the squares to the top of an outdoor table. Set one cup bottom on each square. Add a washer to weigh it down, then pour in some nectar.

Wait patiently for the bees. Which colors do they land on? To keep track, make a table in your notebook. Every ten minutes, check the experiment. Count the number of bees on each color, and write that down next to each color. The next time you check, put your counts in another column of boxes.

At the end of the day, remove the dishes. The next day, do the experiment again. Do the bees visit their favorite square even if no food is on it?

Now confuse the bees. Next to the colored squares, set out gray squares similar in shade to the colored squares. If bees see color, they should land mostly on the colored squares. If they can't, they should visit the gray squares too.

Snail Shelters

Can snails find their way home?

What You'll Need:
Garden with snails, unglazed clay flower pot, water, small rock, acrylic paint, small paintbrush

IF YOU HAVE SNAILS in your garden, try this experiment. Soak an unglazed clay flower pot in water and put it upside-down in the garden—preferably in thick foliage where snails may be present. Prop one side up with a small rock so that snails can get inside. Leave overnight. Check the pot the next day to see if snails are inside. They like cool, moist, dark hiding places.

If the pot has six or more snails, mark each with a small dot of the acrylic paint on the shell. Look in the pot the next day. How many marked snails returned? Are there new ones?

Moth Watching

Attract and study these fascinating night visitors.

What You'll Need:
White sheet or shower curtain, desk lamp, faded tennis ball, string, fruit juice, brown sugar

MOTHS NAVIGATE by moonlight and can be attracted by bright lights. Plants use bright white flowers and heavy fragrances to attract moths, which in turn pollinate the plants. You can draw moths to your own house at night.

WHITE WALL: Get an old white bedsheet or shower curtain and fasten it to an outside wall of your house near an outdoor electrical outlet. Plug in a desk lamp and aim the light beam at the white sheet. Soon you'll see moths congregate on the sheet. Watch for the large, beautiful luna moth, which as an adult has no mouth and cannot feed.

MOTH FOOD: Tie string around a faded tennis ball, leaving a long piece of string for hanging. Dissolve as much brown sugar as you can in a half-cup of fruit juice and soak the tennis ball in the mix. Hang it in a sheltered place. Moths will be attracted by the sweet-smelling fruit juice.

Be an Isopod Expert

Whether you call them pill bugs, sow bugs, or potato bugs, isopods are fun to observe.

What You'll Need:

Jar for collection, garden gloves, foil, lamp, black paper, small desk lamp, sand, two teacups, water

ISOPODS GO BY many names. The round ones that roll up are pill bugs. Those with flat bodies that don't roll are sow bugs. Both may be called wood lice, roly-polies, or potato bugs. Isopods are not bugs or lice—they are crustaceans related to crabs, lobsters, and crayfish.

Take a jar and collect a dozen or so isopods. Wearing gloves, look under flowerpots, beneath big rocks, under logs or boards, and in compost heaps. Put some damp soil or rotted wood in the jar for the animals to hide in.

Now experiment to see what kind of environment isopods prefer. Test one factor at a time to decide what factors are most important to the animals. When you are done with the experiments, return the isopods where you found them.

Make an isopod runway. Cut a large piece of foil and fold it in half for strength. Fold it into box shape measuring about eight inches long, two inches wide, and two inches deep. Then try the following tests.

LIGHT VS. DARK: Cover one-third of the length of the runway with black paper. Shine a small desk lamp on the other end. Place the isopods in the middle and see which end they settle down into.

DRY VS. WET: Put dry sand in one end of the runway. Put wet sand in the other end. Put the isopods in the middle and see which end they prefer.

COLD VS. WARM: Fill one teacup with hot water and the other with cold. Set the runway on the two teacups, one at each end. Put the isopods in the middle and see which end they prefer.

Explore a Rotting Log!

Rotting logs are home to some fascinating creatures.

What You'll Need:

Eroding log,
garden gloves,
magnifying glass,
small clear
plastic jar,
notebook,
pencil

NEXT TIME you are exploring a forest or woodland, look for a decaying log. When you find a soft one, spend time discovering the organisms that live there. Put on your garden gloves and get down on your hands and knees. Using your magnifying glass for a better look at the surface, look to see what lives there. You may find green plants, such moss or small seedlings. You may find insects, such as beetles or termites. There may be other small creatures, such as wood lice and spiders.

If you want a closer look at a small creature, catch it in the jar and observe it. (Let it go when you are done.) Record your discoveries in your notebook. If you don't know the name of something you've found, draw its picture. If the wood is soft, break off a piece to see what kinds of creatures live inside. Termites, ants, and wood-boring beetles often live in logs. Replace the wood when you are done. Record what you find in your notebook.

Now turn the log over and see what lives underneath. The wood may be so rotten that it resembles soil. This is nature's way of recycling. The nutrients that made up the tree's tissue are being returned to the soil for other plants to use. Lots of organisms here are associated with decay, such as millipedes that eat dead plant material, insects that also feed on the dead wood, and earthworms.

Lawn Safari

Take a safari through a patch of grass and see what lives there.

What You'll Need:

Wire coat hanger,
magnifying glass,
notebook,
pencil

SPRING AND SUMMER are the best times to take a lawn safari. You won't see much activity in the winter. Take a wire coat hanger and bend it into a square. Go out on your lawn or in a grassy park and toss the hanger on the grass. Study whatever in the grass is "framed" by the wire. Get down flat on your stomach and have a really close look. Use your magnifying glass as well. Search the grass inch by inch, blade by blade, and find as many animals as you can: earthworms, beetles, grubs, spiders, moths, and anything else.

Jot down what you see in your notebook. If you don't know the name of the animal, draw it. Adult insects have six legs while spiders and their kin have eight, so don't confuse spiders with insects. Take your wire frame and toss it into another patch of grass and do the same thing. Do you find anything different? Try comparing shady grass and sunny grass. Compare thin grass with thick, healthy grass.

Caddisfly Houses

Watch caddisfly nymphs build their cases from material around them.

What You'll Need:
Caddisfly nymphs (collect from a pond),
plastic cups,
natural material for case-building,
such as sand and bits of dead leaves

MOTH-LIKE CADDISFLIES lay their eggs in ponds, marshes, or streams. The nymphs that hatch are aquatic. To protect themselves, they build cases from the materials around them. The nymphs, camouflaged in their cases, can extend their bodies to feed. One kind of caddisfly builds a case resembling a miniature pinecone, bristling with bits of dead leaves. Another builds a long, narrow, cone-shaped case.

Find caddisfly nymphs in clear, shallow water at ponds and streams. You may be able to catch them with your hands. You can also catch them with a dip net (see chapter six, "Pond Dipping"). When you've collected several nymphs, fill some plastic cups with pond water, one for each nymph. Gently remove a nymph from its case and put it in a plastic cup. In one cup, break apart the nymph's old case and see if the nymph will use it. In another, try broken-up dead leaves. In another, try sand, dry grass, or anything else "natural." Time the nymphs to see how long it takes them to build cases. Does it take longer to build a case from one material than another?

Before letting the nymphs go, offer them the same material their original cases were built from and let them make *new* protective cases.

Worming Around
Caddis worms are the larvae of caddisflies. The worms carry around the silken cases the flies live in. The word "caddis" comes from an old European word meaning "cotton wool."

Butterfly Puddles

Give butterflies a helping hand by offering them a drink.

What You'll Need:
Flat pan (such as a pie pan), garden soil, water

Butterflies cannot sip water from ponds or other bodies of water. The surface tension of the water is too strong for their delicate wings. These insects must drink water from nectar and other moist substances. Male butterflies often "puddle" in the summertime at muddy spots which provide butterflies with the water and minerals they need.

You can provide a mud puddle for butterflies to gather in. Fill an old pie pan or other shallow pan nearly to the rim with plain dirt, which is rich in minerals. Add water to make soupy mud. Set your homemade mud puddle out where lots of flowers attract butterflies. Add enough water each day to keep the mud very wet. Watch the puddle over several days. You may see butterflies landing on the mud for a drink.

Mini Pit Trap

Catch small creatures for a close-up view!

What You'll Need:
Garden shovel, one-quart cottage cheese tub or similar container, rocks, board or brick about six inches wide

It's easy to make a miniature trap to catch small insects, spiders, and other soil creatures for observation. First, get permission to dig a hole a bit deeper than your container. Make the hole a half-inch deeper than the tub and a little wider. Set the tub upright in the hole and fill dirt in around the sides. Place four small rocks on the surface near the edges of the hole and set a board or a brick on the rocks.

Now wait for small creatures to fall in your trap. Some will crawl out of the soil and fall in the pit. Others will seek shelter under the board or brick and fall over the edge. Leave the trap out a few hours. Check it in the evening and the next morning. See what happens when you set traps in sunny spots, under a tree, or in a vegetable garden.

Floral Advertising

Flowers are like billboards. But what are they advertising for?

What You'll Need:
Garden with a variety of flowers, notebook, pencil

Look at the different flowers in a large garden. Can you guess what pollinates each kind? If you can't tell, here are some clues. Hummingbirds are attracted to bright red and orange flowers, especially tube-shaped flowers that hang down. Hummingbird flowers offer lots of nectar, but don't have much scent—birds don't have a keen sense of smell. Bees are drawn toward blue and purple flowers that offer lots of nectar and pollen. They also are attracted to white and yellow flowers, even though they don't see yellow all that well.

Why? Because these flowers may have ultraviolet markings that bees see but we can't! Bee flowers may be wide tubes or flat-landing platforms. Butterflies need nectar, and purple, yellow, or red butterfly-pollinated flowers offer plenty. Such flowers are either long tubes that a butterfly's tongue extends into or flat platforms where a butterfly can land and sip nectar. They are often scented; butterflies have an excellent sense of smell.

Moths fly at night, so moth-pollinated flowers are bright white (colors aren't visible at night). Moth-pollinated flowers are often tubular and usually richly scented. Many open only at night, and all offer nectar.

Snail Locomotion

Slow-moving snails are great for studying animal motion.

What You'll Need:
Sheet of clear
plastic or acrylic,
books or a brick,
garden snails,
acrylic paint,
small paintbrush,
notebook,

IF YOU FIND a snail in your garden and turn it over, you'll see that it uses a large, muscular foot to crawl along. But how does this boneless creature get around on one foot? To find out, get a pane of clear plastic or acrylic. Prop one end of the plastic on books or a brick. Position it so that you can look up through the glass from underneath. Now you have a transparent runway for watching snails.

Gather a few snails from the garden. Mark each snail with a small dot of acrylic paint on the shell. Use a different color for each snail to tell them apart. Wet the glass runway and place a snail in the middle. Once it begins moving, watch from underneath. The foot can grip the glass while rippling muscles move it forward. The slime layer lubricates the surface so the foot doesn't get injured. Now put several marked snails in the middle of the glass. Line them up so they face the same direction. Draw their positions in your notebook at the start. Draw their new positions every five minutes. Do the snails move at random, or do you detect patterns in their motion?

If you don't have land snails in your area, try a similar experiment with aquarium snails. Mark some snails with paint, then put them back in the aquarium. Watch them crawl up the sides of the glass and note whether they move in a pattern. If you let algae grow on the sides of the aquarium, snails will leave trails as they eat the algae.

A Sticky Situation

212

Are your spider-senses tingling? Get close to a spider's web.

What You'll Need:
Spiderweb,
bottle of hair spray,
piece of black
construction paper,
safe scissors

IT'S AMAZING how an itsy-bitsy spider builds its fancy web. It's even more incredible to see the finished product up close. Find a spiderweb outside that doesn't have a spider in it. Then spray the web lightly—and carefully—with hair spray. (And don't worry. Spiders build webs quickly, so it isn't a big deal to borrow this spider's home.) You want the web to be stiff, so you might have to spray three or four times.

Now get the construction paper ready behind the web. Carefully cut the strands holding the web to its supports. Catch the web with the construction paper as it comes loose. When the web is on the paper, give it another shot of hair spray so that it sticks to the page. Now, have a look at the way the web is made. It's quite a buggy creation!

Wiggly Worm Farm

215

Old McDonald had some…worms?

What You'll Need:
Large,
wide-mouthed
glass jar,
soil, peat moss,
sand, water, worms,
dead leaves, grass,
paper bag

THEY'RE NOT JUST for fishing anymore! It's easy to watch worms tunnel away when you have a worm farm. First, fill a jar with layers of soil, peat moss, and sand. Then add some water to make the whole thing moist. Now you're ready to head to the garden and dig up some worms.

Once you've found a handful of the little wrigglers, place them in the jar. Put some dead leaves and grass over the top of the worms. Then, lay a paper bag loosely over the top of the jar. Be sure you keep the jar out of the sun because you don't want the worms to get overheated. Check up on the worms every day and water the soil if it is too dry.

Over time, the worms will tunnel through the layers in the jar and you'll be able to watch them in action.

Vacation Variety

Pack your bags, jump in the car, and take off for high adventure! The outdoors offer great getaways and plenty of opportunities for fun. Discover the history of some of the most famous trails, parks, and monuments in our nation. As you go, keep a travel journal filled with narratives of adventures and pictures to remind you of the wonderful places you've been. And, of course, supply yourself with games and other fun things to do on the way. Bon voyage!

Beach in a Bottle

Sift a few memories inside a jar.

What You'll Need:
Clear plastic jar
with lid,
sand,
seashells,
feather,
other beach trivia

EVER LONGED FOR the ocean with none in sight? This beach in a bottle will help "tide" you over between trips. Find a clean, clear plastic jar with a secure lid (a soap-and-water-washed peanut butter jar works well). The next time you hit the beach, gather up half a jar of clean, garbage-free sand. Now, walk the waterline to see what treasures you can find. Are there shells washed up from the ocean floor? A feather from a seabird? A beautiful piece of driftwood? A finely polished piece of beach glass? Drop them in the jar along with the sand. Now securely close the jar and take it home. That bottle of beach will remind you of what you love about the shore and why you want to go back soon.

Tidepooling

Learn about the creatures of the rocky tides.

What You'll Need:

Local tide table, adult partner, notebook and pencil, guidebook to tidal animals of your area

To plan the best time to visit tidepools, get a local tide table from a sporting goods store. Arrive at the tidepools with your adult partner an hour or two before low tide to begin looking as the tide is going out. Sit near the edge of a large pool to observe animals. The longer you look, the more you will see. While actual species will vary at each shoreline, here are some types of animals you're likely to see:

SEA ANEMONES: These simple animals have tentacles around the mouth to trap food. If you gently touch a tentacle, it will feel sticky. This is caused by tiny stingers too small to pierce your skin but able to sting small prey.

SEA STARS: Get flat and watch a sea star in the water moving slowly across the rocks. Can you see the tube feet moving? Sea stars eat mussels, clams, and other shellfish. If you see one with its arms pulled in close and its middle hunched, it's probably eating.

SEA URCHINS: These close relatives of sea stars look like colorful pincushions. Urchins use their spines for defense as well as to scrape rocks to make round holes to hide in. Can you see long tube feet sticking out between the spines? The urchin uses these to move and to pass food to the mouth on the bottom of the animal.

CRABS: Most tidepool crabs are scavengers. Watch them using their claws to feed. Crabs are usually shy, so be patient and watch for them.

Use your notebook to record what you see and approximately where you see it. You'll notice that some animals live in certain areas of the tidal shore. A guidebook to tidepool animals will help you identify actual species, and will help you spot animals found only in your area.

I Spy

Now you can go snorkeling without even getting your face wet!

What You'll Need:
Plastic two-liter ice cream container,
safe scissors,
plastic wrap,
tape,
rubber bands

So WHAT'S THERE to do when you're standing knee-deep in a lake and you're just not up for a swim? Use a "snorkel mask" to check out what's going on below the water's surface!

First, cut out the bottom of a large ice cream tub. Cover this hole (and the sides of the container) with a large piece of plastic wrap. Tape the wrap in place. To make sure the plastic wrap stays put, slide a rubber band over it at the top of the container. Do the same at the other end.

Now you're ready for some underwater exploring! Place the plastic-covered end of your mask in some shallow water. Then, look through the open end of the mask and see if you can catch a glimpse of plants and animals in their watery home. Be sure you don't get any water inside the mask, though, or it'll sink like a stone!

Down By the Sea

She sells seashells...and makes some sculptures, too.
Now you can take a little of the beach home with you!

What You'll Need:
Shovel,
seashells,
pail,
sea water,
plaster of paris,
stick

BEGIN YOUR SCULPTURE by digging a small hole in the sand. Then, place some seashells in the hole so they face up. Fill the pail with sea water and add the plaster of paris. Stir this mixture with the stick until it is smooth.

Now pour the mixture into the hole. Stop filling the hole when the shells are covered. Once you've done this, wait an hour for the plaster to set. When the plaster is dry, pull the sculpture from the sand and take it home with you. It'll make a great addition to your bedroom!

On a Roll 🍃🍃

Get rolling and have some fun with this beach front game!

What You'll Need:
Sand,
shovel,
tennis ball

THIS IS THE PERFECT game for a day at the beach. First, dig one hole in the sand that's big enough for a tennis ball to roll into it. The hole should be about ten feet away from the water.

Then, move back about a foot and dig a row of two holes behind the first hole, making sure they face the water. The holes should be about a foot apart. Now dig three holes in a row another foot behind the two holes. (With each row of holes that you dig, you should be getting further away from the water). Finally, dig four holes in the sand behind the row of three holes. You should now have a triangle-shaped game set up.

After all that hard work, it's time to get rolling! Stand back about 25 to 30 steps from the last row of holes and roll the tennis ball down the beach toward the holes. You're allowed five rolls and you get points for every ball you sink—the hole closest to the water is worth 100 points, each hole in the row with two holes is worth 50 points, each one in the row of three is worth 25 points, and each one in the row of four is worth five points. How many points can you get? Roll with it!

Comb the Beach

Learn why different shoreline organisms live where they do.

What You'll Need:
Tide table,
large ball of string,
adult partner,
brightly colored
bandannas or
scraps of cloth,
notebook,
yardstick,
graph paper

GET A TIDE TABLE from a sporting goods store and look up the next convenient low tide. Arrive at a rocky shoreline an hour before low tide. Find a spot above high tide where you can tie one end of a string to a rock, tree, or a stake. Tie a bandanna to the spot so it's visible. Run the string toward the ocean, stopping as close to the water as you can safely go. Use a rock to hold down the other end of the string.

Starting at the upper end, furthest from the water, write down the most common organisms you see. Work your way slowly down the string. When you see different animals, stop at that spot and mark it with another bandanna. Look back to the first marker and estimate how far down you've dropped in elevation. (Estimate the vertical drop, not how far you've walked.) Continue down the string, adding a bandanna each time you see a different organism.

When you reach the end of the string, wind the string and retrieve the bandannas. As you wind, measure the distance between markers and write that down in your notebook. Get a large piece of graph paper. Let each square represent one foot of shoreline. Use your measurements of vertical distance and the distance between markers to help you draw the shoreline. Then draw in the animals of each zone.

You can use the same mapping techniques to map sandy shores. Rather than using a string, mark a straight line in the sand.

Whale Watching

With luck, you may be able to spot some of the world's largest animals!

What You'll Need:
Warm clothing, binoculars, lunch

IF YOU'RE VISITING a rocky coastline on the Atlantic or Pacific oceans, you may be able to watch for migrating whales. Ask local inhabitants about whales in the area. (Rugged, rocky areas of the Pacific coast are good places to watch for rare Gray whales in late winter and early spring.) Set out early in the morning on a windless, overcast day to a rocky headland that juts out into deep water. Bring binoculars, extra clothing, and snacks or a picnic lunch.

Watch for the blows of spouting whales. A whale blow looks like a puff of smoke at the water's surface. See if you can identify the whale from its blow. You should also be able to see the whale's dark back.

Use your binoculars to look for tail flukes coming out of the water as the whale dives. (This behavior is called "sounding.") The whales will surface hundreds of yards or more from where you saw them dive.

If you're near a lagoon where whales gather, you may spot interesting whale behavior. Gray whales will "spyhop," lifting their snouts out of the water to the level of their eyes. If you're lucky, you may see a whale breech—that is, to leap nearly clear of the water and come down with a splash! No one really knows why whales do this. It may be a courtship ritual, a stress-reliever, a way to shake off parasites, or just plain fun!

Salt Water, Fresh Water

Adding salt to water gives it different properties. Try these fun experiments to learn what a pinch of salt can do!

What You'll Need:
Sea water,
bottled tap water,
two mixing bowls,
bar of pure soap,
potato peeler,
teaspoon,
eggbeater,
dish detergent

NEXT TIME YOU'RE at the seaside, try this experiment to compare salt water to fresh water. First, to look at suds, pour two cups of sea water in one bowl and two cups of tap water in another bowl. Use a potato peeler to shave soap flakes from a bar of pure soap.

Put a teaspoon of flakes in each bowl. Beat with an eggbeater. Which makes better soapsuds, fresh water or salt water? Clean the bowls and do the same experiment with dish detergent. Is there a difference between the kinds of suds produced?

Don't Sweat It

Cool down while you heat up.

What You'll Need:
Towel,
hot summer day

PERSPIRATION IS the human body's natural cooling system. But does it really make a difference? There's one way to find out. The next time a hot day settles on your hometown, take a towel outside and sit in the sun for 30 minutes. For the first 15 minutes, wipe away every drop of sweat you can find as soon as you feel it sneak out. Don't wait an instant. Once those 15 minutes are complete, sit as you normally would, just letting the perspiration pour. Which 15 minutes felt cooler? The answer will give you a whole new perspective on the beauty of a really good sweat. As soon as you're done, go inside and drink some water to rehydrate!

Snag Some Shells

225

Start a collection of treasures and gems from the sea.

What You'll Need:
Bucket for collecting shells,
old newspapers

A SANDY SHORELINE, especially one protected by an offshore reef, is a great place to collect shells in the morning of a calm day at low tide, especially after a storm. Strong winds and high waves will have littered the beach with ocean debris. Carry a bucket and some old newspapers for wrapping up your shells.

When you find a good shell, check it for animals. If it is empty, wrap up the shell in newspaper and add it to your bucket.

How to Skip a Rock

226

Once you get the hang of it, learn the physics of rock-skipping.

What You'll Need:
Flat rocks no larger than your palm

IF YOU'VE EVER wondered how to skip rocks across a surface, here's your chance to learn. First, find a calm body of water. Then, find some flat rocks. Rivers and seashores often have the best skipping rocks. The perfect stone for skipping has rounded edges, is flat on both sides, and fits in the palm of your hand. It can be bigger if it's not too heavy or smaller if it's not too light. Try rocks of different sizes.

For best results, throw sidearm so that the flat side skips across the water as it spins. If you throw just right, the rock should bounce across the surface of the water. To understand how rock skipping works, picture yourself at a swimming pool ready to dive into the water. If you dive just right, your arms and head cut into the water and your body slips through the surface. Now drop a stone edge-first into the water. Like a diver, the rock cuts through the surface instead of bouncing.

Sand Clay

Make souvenirs of your beach vacation!

What You'll Need:
Old double-boiler,
sand, cornstarch,
adult help,
wooden spoon,
hot water,
beach souvenirs,
oven,
spray varnish

To make sand clay, use a double-boiler that you may scratch up. This mixture is very abrasive! Measure one cup of fine sand and a half-cup of cornstarch in the top pan of the double-boiler. Stir together to mix the sand and starch. With adult help, add a half-cup of hot water and stir. Cook over boiling water for ten minutes or until the mixture is thick and the starch is cooked. Don't let the bottom pan go dry.

After the clay cools, make your sculptures. Decorate them with beach treasures like shells and rocks. With adult assistance, bake your sculptures on a baking sheet at 300 degrees until dry. Let your sculptures cool at room temperature for a day or two, then have an adult cover them with spray varnish to keep them from flaking.

Shell Wind Chimes

Seashells can make beautiful music on breezy days.

What You'll Need:
Seashells (especially
clams, mussels,
and oysters),
awl or nut pick,
adult help,
coat hanger,
string or strong
fishing line,
safe scissors

Shells from animals with two shells, such as clams, mussels, oysters, and scallops, make good wind chimes. Pick attractive shells that you don't mind breaking. With an adult's help, take a metal awl or a nut pick and gently work it back and forth in one spot, boring out a small hole for string to run through. The slower you go, the less likely you are to break shells.

Tie each shell to a piece of string and suspend it from your coat hanger. Make sure the shells are close enough together to clink. Suspending some shells lower than others makes a nice pattern. Hang your chimes anywhere that the breeze can catch them. You may want to bring them indoors on very windy days so that the shells don't break.

Your Own Fishing Rod

Assemble fishing tackle and see what you can catch.

What You'll Need:
Sturdy stick four to five feet long, fishing line, safe scissors, fish hook, plastic bobber, bait

YOU DON'T NEED expensive equipment to catch fish. The fish doesn't care if your tackle is store-bought or homemade. The best type of stick for your fishing rod is strong, yet slightly flexible. Bamboo, about one half-inch thick, would be ideal. Find something similar in your own yard or campground.

Let the thick part of the stick be the handle. Tie one end of the fishing line to the handle. Wrap the line in a spiral around the stick until you reach the tip. Tie the line firmly to the tip, but don't cut the line yet. Unroll the line about a foot longer than your stick, and cut it off the roll. You should have a continuous length of fishing line extending from the handle of your stick down to the hook. (That way, if the fishing rod breaks in the middle, you still have the line in your hand.)

Tie a hook to the end of the line. Fasten a bobber to the middle of the line. You'll want to use a ball-shaped red and white bobber with a spring-loaded hook that will fasten it anywhere on the line. Now you're ready to fish! Go with an adult who knows how to fish and what to do with the fish when you catch them. For bait, use worms or other material from a sporting goods store.

What Is Sand?

Sand is more than something to make castles from.
Discover the mysteries in a handful of sand.

What You'll Need:
Beach sand,
white paper,
magnifying glass,
black or dark-
colored paper,
magnet,
small containers,
labels,
pencil or pen

WHERE DOES SAND come from? The sand itself will give you clues. The next time you hit the beach, sprinkle some sand on a sheet of white paper and look at it closely with a magnifying glass. What kinds of particles do you see? How many different colors do you see? Sprinkle some on black or dark-colored paper. Do particles stand out now that were hard to see on white paper? You'll also notice dark particles in the sand. Pass a magnet over your sand sample. Many of the dark particles will stick to the magnet. These are iron-rich minerals, such as magnetite. If you are patient, you can try sorting the sand particles into separate piles.

Sand is made of tiny rock fragments eroded by water. Some of your sand grains are the same color as nearby rocks. You may find a lot of light-colored or even clear particles. Many of these are quartz, a mineral high in silica. Because most sand has a lot of quartz, it is used to manufacture glass.

Real Sand Castles

Did you know that sand is a big part of what makes most buildings? Both glass and concrete, as well as paper and many chemicals, are manufactured from sand.

If you visit beaches in different areas, start a sand collection. Find small, clear bottles or plastic containers. (Some film-developing shops will give you clear film canisters for free.) Scoop a sample of sand from the beach into a container. Label and date the container. If you have friends living on or visiting other coastlines or sandy shores, ask them to send you sand for your collection.

Sand Memory Game

Here's a great game for two that only requires a good memory!

What You'll Need:
Beach,
rocks or shells,
beach towel

SIT BACK TO BACK on the sand and draw a grid. Decide ahead of time how big to make your grid. You might start with a grid 16 squares large (four squares per side), then make it bigger as you get better. Have your friend turn away while you set out rocks on your grid. You can only put one rock on each square, but you don't have to put a rock on every square. Once you've created your rock pattern, cover it with a towel.

Uncover your grid and let your friend look at it for 15 seconds, then re-cover the grid with the towel. Your friend now has to duplicate the pattern on his or her own grid. When your friend is done, lift the towel and see how close he or she got. Switch roles and let your friend lay out a pattern. Change the rules as you get better at the game. You might allow more than one rock per square. You could use different markers, such as shells, rocks, and twigs, or make bigger grids.

Stay out of the Tide

Remember when you're near a roaring tide to wear sturdy shoes with non-slip soles. never turn your back on the ocean, because "sneaker" waves can wash away unwary visitors. And always have an adult with you.

Building Sand Castles

Build your own kingdom in the sand.
How long can it withstand the tides?

What You'll Need:

Digging tools (stick, small shovel, big metal spoons), pails of many sizes, plastic food containers of various sizes, beach debris

SAND CASTLES ARE FUN. You can make them as small and simple or as large and complex as you like. If you start your castle soon after high tide, you will have all day before the tide returns to sweep your work away. Find a place on wet sand near the high-tide mark and begin. Mark the size of your castle. Use a stick to draw a ring in the sand. With shovels, spoons, or other digging equipment, dig a moat around the castle and pile the sand in the middle of your circle.

Wet the sand with sea water until it can stick together. Pat it down firmly, then use your digging tools to carve it. Cut away paths and courtyards. The remaining high mounds will form your towers. Leave a wall around the castle on the inside of the moat. Sculpt towers and chimneys, using buckets and plastic containers as molds. Fill the container with damp sand, pack it down, turn it over, and slap the sides until the molded sand comes out.

Gather up shells, sticks, kelp, or other debris and construct castle inhabitants. Bulbs of kelp can be the heads of knights and maidens. Driftwood sticks tied together can be horses. Colored pebbles and beach glass (check for sharp edges) might be jewels in a treasure house.

By the time the tide rolls in, your castle should resist the waves unless it is submerged completely. Return the next day and see if your castle survived.

Forever Fish

No one will question your fish stories if you preserve your prize fish forever in plaster.

What You'll Need:
Fish,
modeling clay,
plaster of paris,
mixing container
for plaster, spoon,
acrylic paints,
paintbrush,
spray acrylic,
adult help, hot glue
or cement (optional)

YOU MAY CATCH a fish so big that you'd love to see it preserved and mounted on the wall so you can show it off to your friends. With some plaster and clay, you can! Clean your fish and leave the head on. Lay it out flat in a pan. Set it in a freezer overnight and let it freeze. The next day, remove the fish from the freezer. Roll out a slab of modeling clay a little bigger and a little thicker than your fish. Press the fish firmly into the clay. Gently pull it out and see if you like the mold you've made. If there are air bubbles or imperfections, knead the clay, roll it out, and try again.

When you've got a mold you like, put the fish back in the freezer. Mix some plaster in a container until it is about as thick as heavy cream. Pour the plaster slowly into the mold. Try to avoid making air bubbles. Let the plaster dry several hours, then remove it from the mold. Let the plaster dry completely overnight before attempting to remove any clinging bits of modeling clay. Once your plaster fish dries, decorate it with acrylic paints. Use the frozen fish as a color model to ensure that your plaster fish looks as real as possible. After the paint dries, spray it with clear acrylic coating. If you like, use hot glue (with adult help) or contact cement to mount your plaster fish to a wall plaque.

Kite Fishing
Kites have been used for centuries in Asia for fishing. A hook and bait are attached to a kite, which is then lowered into the water. Kites get to hard-to-reach places, and since they sail softly, you can sink a baited hook into the water without scaring the fish.

The Great Outdoors

Hit the trail and discover the wonders of the great outdoors! Whether you head to the mountains, desert, beach, lake, forest, or just your own backyard, you'll find plenty of places to hike or pitch a tent. Learn to camp like a pro, leaving no sign you've been there. Walk in the footsteps of the early explorers. Find out how good food can taste when you cook it outdoors over a fire or a camp stove. And at all times, be a good outdoor citizen. Clean up after yourself, and don't pester or feed the animals. Happy trails!

On the Right Track

234

Track down a few facts.

What You'll Need:
Notebook, pencil or pen, books on animal tracks from the library

WE LOVE HIKING. But who hikes with us? What animals call that natural territory home? If you keep your eyes carefully trained to the ground, you might find out. Watch for animal tracks as you go. If you find tracks too difficult to spot, look for animal droppings (even animals have to process the food they eat—it's all part of nature).

If there *are* droppings, tracks won't be far behind. Take out your notebook and do your best to draw the tracks you find. When you get home, check to find out who might have left them behind. It's fun to know you're never really alone.

Fire Building

Here's how to build a safe campfire to toast marshmallows over.

What You'll Need:
Shovel,
small bits of
flammable material
for tinder,
thin wood for
kindling,
larger wood for fuel,
matches,
bucket of water

LEARN TO LAY and light a fire safely before trying it in the woods. Practice in your fireplace, but NEVER light fires without an adult. When you gather firewood, only pick up what you see on the ground. Don't cut down living trees or break off branches for your fire.

Use an existing fire pit if possible. If there is no fire pit, clear a safe area. Remove any flammable material within a six-foot radius of your fire. Dig down to mineral soil. Have a bucket of water handy to put out the fire later. Start with a fist-sized wad of dry tinder (any material catching fire when lit with a match). Wood shavings, dry pine needles, dry moss, pocket lint, and bundled dry grass make good tinder. Then build a small log cabin of pencil-thin kindling around the tinder. Lay some sticks on top of the cabin but leave space for air flow.

Lay three or four one-inch diameter sticks of fuel wood on top of the kindling. Light the tinder. When it catches fire, gently blow on it to encourage the flame. Add more fuel wood when the fire is burning. If you're cooking over the fire, wait until there is a good bed of coals. When you're finished, pour water on the fire until the ashes are cool to the touch. Never leave a site or go to sleep without putting the fire out.

Finding Big Foot

"Sasquatch" is real—at least if you use your imagination.

What You'll Need:
Garden gloves,
paper,
pencil or pen

COULD THE MYSTERIOUS monster "Big Foot" be more than a myth? Hike through your local wilderness and search for fun and furry clues—even if you don't quite believe. Keep your eyes peeled for fun clues that could have been left by Big Foot. Put on some garden gloves and forage around. See a clump of hair? Grab it—it might be a piece of Big Foot's fur. Spy a tiny piece of bone? Maybe that was Big Foot's afternoon snack. Is that a cave you see in the distance? Make a note of it. It may be Big Foot's home. When you get back to camp, write down everything you saw and make up a campfire story about all the things you've found. You'll have fun trying to scare each other silly!

Outdoor Alphabet

Go by the letter for outdoor fun.

What You'll Need:
Family or friends

SEARCHING FOR an outdoor alphabet can be your ticket to better observational skills as well as a whole lot of hiking fun. As you hike the trail with your parents and friends, call out the letters of the alphabet one by one. If you see an apple, say, "Apple" out loud and move on to the letter "B." If your father sees a bug, you all move on to the letter "C." If your mother sees a canary, you all move on to the letter "D." This is a team game full of team spirit, so cheer each other on. Before you know it, you'll be where you wanted to be—and you will have had lots of fun along the way.

Campsite Bingo

Try this game B-4 you hit the trail.

What You'll Need:
Paper,
pencil or pen,
edible game pieces
(like popcorn,
animal crackers, or
red-hot candies)

THIS IS A GREAT WAY to celebrate the great outdoors—and BINGO is its name-o. It's not traditional bingo. It's a fill-in-the-blank game that has more to do with what you see than what someone says. Take a blank piece of paper and write B-I-N-G-O in big letters all the way across it. Now, grab a partner. (The buddy system is especially important in the American wilderness.) Staying close enough to camp to hear each other, search for something that begins with a "B." It can be a bug, a piece of birch, a baseball you packed, or anything else that starts with "B." Do the same with the rest of the letters in the word "BINGO," using the game pieces on the paper to help you keep track of what you've found. The first team to find all five objects wins the game.

Shoe In, Shoe Out

Which shoes are best for the environment?

What You'll Need:
Sneakers,
variety of ordinary
yard plants,
soft dirt,
hiking boots

WE THINK HIKING boots are best for hitting the dusty trail. But this experiment shows that sneakers could be healthier for the wild and wonderful plants you see along the way. Lay out small cuttings from six or seven of your favorite yard plants (after getting permission from mom and dad). Now take normal steps over those plants with your sneaker-covered feet. How do the plant bits look? Did they survive the "hike"?

Now slip into some hiking boots and repeat the experiment. Are your greens squashed? Hiking boots are much tougher on plant life than ordinary sneakers. So the next time you go for a hike off the beaten trail, do the indigenous plant life a favor and wear your favorite sneaks.

Hiking Back in Time

Try "the good old days" on for size.

What You'll Need:
Large square of
cloth,
walking stick,
beef jerky,
water,
dried fruit

WHILE GROWNUPS call hiking "getting back to nature," today's hiking supplies make it a pretty modern activity. So why not take yourself back in time the next time you hit the rugged trail? Pack the way the pioneers might have done. Instead of a fanny pack, grab a square of cloth and tie it around a walking stick. Forget the snack bars and sports drinks. Pack some beef jerky, water, and dried fruit. Think about hiking as a means of transportation, rather than something to do just for fun. You'll come back to the present with a whole new appreciation.

Let's Have a Cookout!

Cooking on an outdoor grill is easy and fun.

What You'll Need:
Grill, old newspaper
or wax-based
fire starters,
charcoal briquets,
matches or butane
lighter, hot dogs,
hamburgers,
serving dish,
spatula

TO MAKE A CHARCOAL FIRE, place crumpled newspaper (or two wax-based fire-starting cubes) in the middle of the barbecue. Pile charcoal briquets loosely over the paper. Leave space between the briquets and the grill. Have an adult help you use a long match or a butane charcoal starter to light the paper. Once the charcoal is burning, put the lid on the grill to hold the heat in while the charcoal burns to coal. (A homemade grill has no lid, so you'll have to wait a bit longer.)

Once you have a good bed of coals, grill something easy, like hot dogs—all they need is to be heated. Set them on the grill and let them cook until they sizzle, turning them once. Once they're hot, put them in a serving dish. Next, shape hamburger meat into patties about a half-inch thick and place on the grill. Cover and let them cook about five minutes. Turn with a long-handled spatula and finish cooking on the other side.

Know Your Poisons!

Learn to recognize plants that will give you a rash if touched.

What You'll Need:
Garden gloves, drawings or photos of poisonous plants, posterboard or large construction paper, home medical book, construction paper, safe scissors, glue

BEFORE YOU GO HIKING in the woods, you'd better know what plants have oils that could give you an itchy rash. Help yourself and your fellow hikers by knowing how to recognize the following plants:

POISON IVY has three pointed, shiny leaflets; in the summer, poison ivy may have white berries. Found over most of the United States, ivy may cross with poison oak where the two plants are found near each other. **POISON OAK** is like poison ivy, but the leaves are more rounded and resemble the leaves of a white oak. The plant may be a shrub or a tree-climbing vine. Found mostly on the West Coast, usually in forests and on sunny, dry slopes. It's also found in disturbed places. **POISON SUMAC** has seven to nine pointed leaflets. The leaves are shiny and it, too, may have white berries. Found mostly in the eastern United States.

If poisonous plants live in your area, find a specimen in the wild. ALWAYS WEAR GARDEN GLOVES. Photograph or draw it as accurately as you can. Use a home medical guide to learn proper treatment for contact with poisonous plants. Make a poster with this information using cut-out letters from construction paper.

Camping In

Find camping fun in your own backyard!

What You'll Need:
Tent, sleeping bag, charcoal grill (with adult help)

CAMPING OUT miles from home might seem a little scary for beginners. Camping in can be a great first step. Set up everything you'd normally use for outdoor camping and do your best to pretend you're really in the wild. Cook on the grill (with adult help). No TV, no electricity. (You can use the bathroom facilities inside; that's the only shortcut you'll take.) This is Camping 101, just to get you ready for the real thing.

The Comforts of Home—Outdoors!

How to keep clean out in the wild without harming the environment.

What You'll Need:
Shovel, biodegradable toilet paper (from a camping supplier), plastic garbage bags, biodegradable soap (from a camping supplier), bandanna

HERE'S HOW to take care of hygiene in the wildnerness without polluting. To make a one-day **LATRINE,** scoop a shallow "cat hole" in the dirt with your heel for solid waste and urine. Bury the waste when you are done. NEVER use waterways as toilets! For overnight camping, dig a latrine (around ten inches deep) behind some bushes away from camp. Leave dirt and a trowel or shovel by the latrine to cover waste immediately. Keep biodegradable toilet paper in a waterproof container.

To make a **GARBAGE DISPOSAL,** burn fruit peels and plate scrapings in a campfire (if you have one). Put other trash in plastic bags and suspend them from tree limbs. Take them when you leave. Don't bury your garbage, or animals will dig it up later. For **DISHWASHING,** wipe the pot out with a paper towel and burn the towel in your campfire (or put it in your garbage bag to throw out). Fill the pot with water and heat it. Add a drop of biodegradable soap. Let the water boil, then remove the pot. Let it cool, then swish the pot clean with a bandanna. Dig a shallow hole outside of camp to dump the soapy water into. Don't dump soapy or dirty water into streams, lakes, or rivers.

What You Really Need
What are the camping essentials? According to experts, always bring water, a compass, maps, a daypack, food, extra clothing, matches, a first aid kit, a flashlight and sunscreen, bathroom paper, a mirror to signal with, and rain gear.

How to Get Found

Getting lost in the woods is scary.
Make a kit to help you get found fast!

What You'll Need:

Aluminum foil, map, waterproof carrying bag, large plastic garbage bag, mylar emergency blanket, whistle, extra sweater or jacket, unbreakable mirror, granola bars, water bottle, compass

Common sense can keep you from getting lost in the outdoors, and get you found even if you do. Before you go, press aluminum foil against the sole of your hiking shoe to make an impression of the tread. Search parties use impressions like these to find a missing person's footprints. Next, study a map of the area you'll be in and learn the route. Give a copy of the map and your schedule to someone at home.

Then make a "get found" kit to carry in a waterproof bag. Include a large plastic garbage bag with a ten-inch hole in one corner, a mylar emergency blanket, a whistle, an extra sweater or jacket, an unbreakable mirror, granola bars, and extra water. Carry your map and compass in your hand or a convenient pocket. Check the map frequently, stay with your group at all times, and ALWAYS stay on the trail. When camping, don't wander from your site.

If you get lost, stay calm, stay in one place, and let rescuers find *you*. Establish a base camp. Choose a tree and stay close to it. Blow your whistle often, and flash your mirror in all directions to attract attention. If it's cold, put on the extra sweater or jacket. Sit by your tree and pull the trash bag over your head. (Your face should stick out of the hole you've cut.) Wrap the blanket around you for extra warmth and visibility. Blow that whistle. If you are cold, move around, but stay near the tree, which can be a windbreak. If it rains, you can stay dry in the trash bag!

How to Use a Compass

Learn to use a map and compass to find your way outdoors.

What You'll Need:

Orienteering-style compass with degree markings (such as a Silva compass), map of your local area or area of interest

IF YOU LEARN to use a map and compass, you'll be less likely to get lost in the wilderness. To align the compass, read the directions for the compass and learn which end of the needle points north. Turn the compass until the north arrow on the compass' face is aligned with the north end of the pointer. You are now aligned "north." Observe the letters on the compass: N is north, E is east, S is south, W is west. You'll also find northeast, southeast, southwest, and northwest. Next, look at the numbers. These are degrees, another form of measuring compass direction.

Turn and face any direction. Hold one hand out flat and place the compass on your palm. Point the arrow on the baseplate in the direction you're facing. Turn the dial on the compass until the north-facing arrow is aligned with the pointer. Now read the degree mark that the index line crosses. This is your direction in degrees.

Rules of Thumb

There are three important mottos to remember when you hike in the wilderness: "Leave only footprints. Take only memories. Kill only time." Observing those guidelines will protect the trails for generations to come.

To find your bearing, place the map on the ground and find where you want to start and end. Place the compass so that it matches both points. Turn the dial until "north" points the same direction as the north indicator on the map. The index on the baseplate should now line up with the correct bearing on the dial. Turn the compass in the correct direction.

Orienteering Games

247

Play outdoor games that challenge your map and compass skills.

What You'll Need:
Orienteering-style compass with degree markings (such as a Silva compass), map of your local area or area of interest, flag

IF YOU KNOW how to use a map and compass, you're ready for new challenges. These games are great to play with friends, fellow campers, or youth groups. Try the beeline game. Stand on a starting mark. Use a compass to find the exact bearing of a certain landmark within a few minutes' walk. Make sure there are obstacles between the landmarks and the starting point. Measure the distance in paces.

Have all players begin at the same starting point. Give each player or team of players the bearing of one of the landmarks. Tell them to go a certain number of paces in a straight line in their given direction. Don't tell them what landmark to aim for. On your signal, the teams set out. It's up to each team to cope with obstacles, but make sure to be safe and set rules regarding safety and private property. When the teams reach what they think is the destination, they should wave a flag as a signal. Award points to those closest to the landmark.

Knee-High Hike

228

Hiking is only human, until you try this trick.

What You'll Need:
Long, sturdy pants, protective gloves

IF YOU WANT to see hiking from a whole new point of view, why not fall to your knees? Take your next short hike on all fours, as would a puma, chipmunk, or hyena, and see how your perspective is bound to change. Be sure to wear pants sturdy at the knees and gloves to protect your hands. Then head for the trail. What do you see from this animal-like position? What do you smell? How do you feel? Do you begin to get a sense of how vulnerable some creatures of the wild might be? It's a whole new world.

Historical Trails

What paths of history are near your hometown?

What You'll Need:
Guidebooks to local trails (check your library), composition book, pencil

HISTORY WILL COME alive when you walk in the footsteps of famous explorers, pioneers, or early Native Americans. Our Historical Trail and Scenic Trail systems began in the 1920s as citizens began piecing together hiking trails on historical routes. It was their vision that led to the National Trail System Act of 1968. All the trails are for foot traffic only, and most of them cross several states.

Check the following list to see which Historical Trails are near you. Make a trail notebook. Keep a record of the trails you've been on. Include some history of the trails in your book and mark the segments you hike. Our trails are:

Iditarod National Historic Trail (Alaska)

Juan Bautista de Anza National Historic Trail (Mexico and Southwest U.S.)

Lewis and Clark National Historic Trail (Missouri to Oregon)

Mormon Pioneer National Historic Trail (Illinois to Utah)

Nez Perce National Historic Trail (Idaho, Wyoming, Montana)

Oregon National Historic Trail (Missouri to Oregon)

Overmountain Victory National Historic Trail (Tennessee to North Carolina)

Pony Express National Historic Trail (Missouri to California)

Santa Fe National Historic Trail (Missouri to Santa Fe, Mexico)

Trail of Tears National Historic Trail (Georgia to Oklahoma).

Poison Warning

When you walk the trails, DON'T believe the dangerous myth that you can become immune to poison ivy by eating it. People who have tried it have landed in the hospital! If you come in contact with poison ivy or poison oak, use soap and water to wash the oils off right away.

Camp Cooking Gadgets

It's fun to make useful "gadgets" for your outdoor kitchen.

What You'll Need:
Unpainted coat hangers, heavy-duty aluminum foil, wire cutters (with adult help), pliers

RATHER THAN BUYING things you might only need once, see how inventive you can be with wire and foil. To make a **MEAT FORK,** cut the hook off a stiff wire coat hanger and straighten the wire. Bend the middle of the wire around a thick stick to form a loop. Twist the stick while holding the two strands with pliers. Leave about four inches of wire untwisted. Separate these to form two tines. Remove the stick from the loop in the handle. If the handle sags, wire it to a straight stick.

LADLE: Begin as you did for the meat fork, but leave six-inch ends. Bend the ends around a tin can or flashlight to form a circle. Wrap the overlapping ends of wire around each other. Shape the bowl of the ladle from foil. Push the bowl through the wire circle. Leave plenty of foil for the overlap, and fold the overlap under the bowl of the ladle.

BISCUIT PAN: Straighten a wire coat hanger. Fold the wire into a square and twist the ends together. Use any extra wire to form a loop. Using the wire square as a pattern, form a box from two layers of foil. Leave several inches for overlap. Place the foil box in the wire square and fold the overlap down and under the edges of the box. Set cut biscuits in the pan. Sprinkle on a layer of smooth ashes. Set the biscuit pan on the coals. Cover with foil. Check often.

Leave it Alone

Capture the magic of nature without leaving a trace.

What You'll Need:
Hard surface
(book, cardboard,
magazine),
white paper,
crayons (some
with the paper
peeled away)

As you WANDER the wonders of nature and the great outdoors, you're bound to see dozens of things you'd love to remember and dozens of images you'd love to take home. But in many natural parks and outdoor centers, it's against the rules to pick a flower or even a single leaf. This project will help you collect memories without hurting a single petal.

When you see a leaf, gently press it between a hard surface (like a piece of cardboard or a book) and a plain piece of white paper. Now, take a crayon with the paper peeled away and lay it on its side on the surface of the paper. Rub gently across the paper and leaf. Before you know it, you'll have a "copy" of the ridges and textures of that special leaf.

Flowers don't hold up well to rubbings, but you can take the time to sketch a picture of the blossoms you see. Be sure to make notes about where you saw the flower and what made it special to you.

Mini-Munchy Cookout

Sometimes good things come in small packages.

What You'll Need:
Mini-hot dogs,
mini-marshmallows,
pointed sticks
(be careful!)

Everyone knows that cooking hot dogs and marshmallows is a campsite tradition. Why not do your roasting in miniature, just for a "little" added fun? Instead of stocking up on standard-size frankfurters, why not pack a bundle of tiny little dogs? Slip these bite-sized snacks on a thin stick and heat them up over an open fire. Be careful not to burn yourself and make sure you have an adult with you to oversee the cookout. After the weenies, you can roast tiny marshmallows!

Dinner On a Stick

All you need is a long, pointy stick to cook up some great food!

What You'll Need:
Long, slender hardwood sticks (maple, oak, alder, or ash are good), pocket knife (with adult help!), ingredients for individual recipes

Have an ADULT help you cut pencil-thick cooking sticks about two and a half feet long. Carve one end of the sticks to a point. Slip the food onto the point and push it back so that an inch or so of stick pokes out the other side. Cook the food over a good bed of hot coals (not flames, which will just scorch it). Hold the food horizontally over the coals and turn frequently until done.

HOT DOGS AND SAUSAGES: Push the stick through the hot dog or sausage lengthwise, or it may break in half and fall in the fire. Roast over coals, turning constantly, until sizzling. For **KEBABS,** cut meat into one-inch square cubes. Cut small onions in quarters. Cut potatoes, carrots, or bell peppers into chunks about an inch across. Slip chunks of meat and vegetables onto your stick. Roast over the coals until the meat is done.

Food in Foil

Great recipes for the coals of a campfire or on an outdoor grill!

What You'll Need:
Outdoor grill (charcoal or gas) or campfire, heavy-duty aluminum foil, ingredients for individual recipes

Make **CHICKEN AND RICE** by placing two raw chicken breasts on a large piece of foil. Mix one can of condensed mushroom soup with two thirds of a cup of uncooked instant rice. Seal the foil. Cook over coals for about 20 minutes, turn, then cook 20 minutes longer.

For grilled **CORN ON THE COB,** husk an ear of corn. Spread with butter, sprinkle with salt and pepper, and wrap tightly in foil. Place on coals and grill for ten minutes, turning occasionally. To make **EGGS** in foil, shape a square of foil over the end of a soup can to form a cup. Slide the cup from the can and break an egg in it. Set the cup on a grill for 10 minutes or on coals for three minutes. Top with grated cheese.

Food For the Trail

Next time you go on a long hike, pack
some of these fun foods along with you.

255

What You'll Need:
Ingredients for
individual recipes

FOOD FOR HIKING should be easy to carry and shouldn't make a mess. Pack your food in moisture-proof containers, such as plastic sandwich boxes, that will keep sandwiches from getting crushed and will contain any spills. Always carry plenty of drinking water. (Don't trust open water sources along the trail.) Try these recipes as a change of pace from the ordinary sandwich-and-fruit lunch:

HOT DOGS: Before leaving on a hike, fill a wide-mouthed vacuum bottle with hot water. Add a hot dog and seal the bottle. Put a bun in a sandwich bag and condiments in small containers. When you're ready for lunch, your hot dog should be hot.

INSTANT TACO: Pack hot, cooked taco meat in a wide-mouthed insulated vacuum bottle. Fill a plastic lunchbox with tortilla chips or a taco shell and sprinkle on grated cheese. If you like, pack chopped tomatoes or lettuce in a separate container. At lunch time, scoop the meat onto the chips, add tomatoes and lettuce, and eat from the chip container.

WALKING SALAD: Cut off the top of an apple. Carefully cut out the core almost to the bottom. Scoop out the pulp of the apple and mix it with two large spoonfuls of cottage cheese, some chopped nuts, and raisins. Stuff the mixture back into the apple shell. Replace the top and use toothpicks to hold it on. You can eat the salad and the container too!

No-Utensil Food

Let your campfire burn down, then try these no-pan recipes!

What You'll Need:
Hot coals,
ingredients for
recipes,
string,
safe scissors,
metal bucket,
salt water

ORANGE CUP BREAKFAST: Halve an orange and scoop out the fruit. Leave the peel intact. Break an egg in one orange cup. Measure mix for one muffin into the other cup and add water. (The batter should half-fill the cup.) Set the cups on hot coals for 10 minutes.

ROASTED GREEN CORN: Peel the husks back, leaving the cobs attached at the bottom, and remove the silks. Replace the husks to cover the ears and tie in place. Soak the ears for 15 minutes in a clean bucket of salt water. Set the ears upright against a rock near the coals. Turn until all sides are slightly browned. Remove the husks and eat right away!

CAVEMAN POTATOES: With a stick, push aside some coals in the fire. Drop a clean potato in the gap and cover with ashes and coals. Bake 30 minutes. Scrape the coals and roll the potato on to a plate. Allow to cool, then brush off the ashes. Eat by scooping the potato from the jacket.

Make an Outdoor Grill

Outdoor cooking is even more fun when you make your own grill!

What You'll Need:
Permission,
grating (from a
camping supply
store), shovel, bricks
or cement blocks,
sand, charcoal

On BARE SOIL, away from flammable materials, make a rectangle in the dirt as long as your grating and four inches wider. Use this outline to dig a rectangular, flat-bottomed pit two inches deep. With help, set the bricks flat on the short sides of the pit. Stack up a second layer of bricks. When making the second layer, overlap the bricks to make a stronger stack. The second layer won't be as long as the first, but should be as wide as the grill. Line the pit with at least an inch of sand. This will insulate the ground underneath to prevent fires. When you're ready to cook, remove the grating and pour your charcoal on the sand.

Easy Tent

Who needs expensive stuff?

What You'll Need:
Tarp, large sheet of plastic, or old shower curtain, narrow rope or clothesline, tent stakes, four small rocks, heavy twine, heavy safe scissors

IT'S FUN TO CAMP in the summer. You don't even need an expensive tent if you're just going out for a night in fair weather. This easy shelter will keep off a light rain, but if it begins pouring, you'll want to go in a heavier tent or in the family car!

Stretch a rope between two trees, posts, or any other stationary objects. The rope should be about three or four feet off the ground—lower, if you have a smaller tarp. Drape the tarp over the rope so that it hangs evenly on both sides. If the tarp has metal grommets in the corners, stretch the corners out and hold them down with tent stakes. (If you are using a sheet of plastic or an old shower curtain, wrap each corner over a small rock and tie with twine.) Leave enough twine to tie to a tent stake. If you just poke the stake through the plastic, it will tear.

Make sure the sides of your tent are as tight as you can make them so they won't flap in the wind. If possible, face the tent so the wind strikes the side instead of blowing through. Now, prepare your bed. Put down a foam camping mat to sleep on. (Several layers of thick blankets will work, too.) Air mattresses are cushiony but cold to sleep on. If you use an air mattress, cover it with a foam pad or heavy blankets. The trick to staying warm at night is to have something warm between you and the ground, since the cold ground draws heat away from your body.

Long-Ago Tents

The word "tent" comes from an old Latin word meaning "to stretch." In older times, fabrics were used to shelter people from the elements. Now, our tents are made of much more water-resistant material.

Camp Desserts

Give your meal a big finish with fun, do-it-yourself desserts!

What You'll Need:
Ingredients for recipes, outdoor grill or campfire

BANANA BOATS: Peel a banana, then push your thumb in one end until the three lengthwise "sections" separate. Remove the "section" near the inside curve or use a spoon to scoop it out. Fill the cavity with tiny marshmallows and chocolate chips. Wrap the banana in foil and place in the coals until the sweets melt (five to 10 minutes).

S'MORES: Break a graham cracker in half and place a one-inch square of chocolate on it. Toast a marshmallow until it turns golden, then place the marshmallow on the chocolate and set the other cracker square on it. Hold in place and slide the stick out. Squish together and eat!

BAKED APPLE: Cut the core from an apple but leave the bottom intact. Fill the hollow space with brown sugar, cinnamon, and raisins (if you like). Wrap in foil and place in the coals. Let the apple bake about 30 minutes.

Trail Markers

Lay a trail for others to follow using trail markers.

What You'll Need:
Available natural materials such as sticks, rocks, and grass

TRAIL MARKERS can come from any natural material—sticks, bunches of grass, or rocks. If one hiking group heads down the trail before the others, the lead group can leave markers to describe which fork in the trail to take. To play a **TRAIL MARKER GAME**, have one person or group lay out a trail for the rest of the group. The trail shouldn't be complex, nor should markers be hidden. The person laying the trail uses different types of markers. The person or group following must walk the trail without using maps or diagrams. Use this game to practice memorizing and spotting skills.

Solar Still

In an emergency, you can get fresh water from the soil!

What You'll Need:
Shovel,
flowerpot,
clear plastic sheet,
rocks

AFTER GETTING PERMISSION, dig a hole several feet deep or until you hit moisture. Set a flowerpot in the bottom of the hole. Lay a sheet of clear plastic over the hole. Weigh the edges with heavy rocks and seal the hole with dirt. Set a rock in the middle of the sheet, over the pot, so that the plastic leans in. Water will bead on the plastic sheet. Heat from the sun, trapped in the hole, makes water evaporate from the damp soil. The water condenses on the sheet then drips into the pot.

If you are lost and you can't find damp soil, cut some plant material and drop it in the bottom of the hole. Any moisture in the plants will evaporate, condense on the plastic, and drip into the pot. While you wait, stay in the shade to conserve body moisture. Even if you live far from a desert, try this in your yard. It could be a good science fair project.

Greetings on the Trail

Say "hi" in the dirt.

What You'll Need:
Stick,
water

IN EARLIER TIMES, explorers marked trees and rocks to help them retrace their steps or communicate with other explorers. In today's campgrounds, carving trees and rocks isn't a very good idea. But you can etch a message in the dirt for the next hiker. Use a sharp stick to carve your comment—your name, a message, a warning about a slippery rock— into the soil. If the dirt is too hard, add a trickle of fresh, clean water (water with no leaves or dirt in it) and then carve your hello. It's one way to reach out to other outdoor lovers without damaging the natural setting you came to see.

Solar Cooker

263

Try using the power of the sun to heat up a hot dog!

What You'll Need:
Cardboard box,
safe scissors,
masking tape,
shiny aluminum foil,
heavy-duty plastic
wrap,
hot dog

THIS SOLAR COOKER uses reflective surfaces and the "greenhouse" princi-
ple to generate heat from sunlight. It won't cook raw food, but can
heat a hot dog. Cut the top flaps off a medium-sized cardboard box
and turn it on its side. Cut the sides at an angle from the bottom corner
up to about the middle of the top. Use the cardboard scraps to make a
slanted interior tilting from the top to the back corner. Hold it together
with masking tape. Cut a hole in the back of the box to reach through.
Cut a door in the back of the slanted interior and hinge it with masking
tape. Use masking tape to reinforce weak points in the box.

Line the inside of the box with foil, making a smooth, reflective surface.
Cut around the door carefully and use loops of tape to attach the foil to
the door. Cover the front of the box with clear, heavy-duty plastic wrap,
pull the wrap tight, and tape it in place. Set your cooker in bright, hot
sun so that the sun hits the plastic-wrapped front. Put your hot dog on
a square of foil inside the cooker. Check after 15 minutes. Turn the box
to follow the sun. Try moving the reflective portion to different angles.

Give Me Some Direction

262

Which way is which in the dark?

What You'll Need:
Friend,
open space,
blindfold,
compass

DO YOU HAVE a good sense of direction? Here's how to find out. Grab a
friend, a blindfold, and a compass. Go to a wide-open space where
you can walk in all directions (and fall down if you get dizzy). Have
your friend wrap the blindfold around your eyes, then, with you facing
north, have him spin you three times. Now, he should ask you to walk two
steps to the north...then south...then east...then west. Make sure he
uses a compass to check which way you go.

Super Sports and Games

"Hey, can you come out and play?" You'll never have to wonder what to do next time friends come calling when you have this chapter full of games to choose from. Try out some great old-fashioned games like kick-the-can, hopscotch, or marbles. Learn some new ways to play hide-and-seek. Once you've played these games and discovered your favorites, try making up your own rules to take advantage of the unique features of your neighborhood.

Make a Run for It

On your mark, get set, GO! See how fast you can make it through a backyard obstacle course.

What You'll Need:
Hula hoops, garden hose, lawn chairs, wading pool, apples, garbage bags, soccer ball, stopwatch or watch with second hand

To SET UP your course, look around the house for things you can use. You'll be surprised at what you can do with everyday objects. For example, set up a zig-zag row of hula hoops to hop through on one leg. Roll out the garden hose so it makes a winding path for you to jump back and forth over until you reach the next obstacle. How about a row of lawn chairs to crawl under without knocking any over?

After you've squirmed through the lawn chairs, race around a full wading pool three times and bob for the apple. Next, have a garbage bag ready. Jump in feet first and hop to the next obstacle. Kick a soccer ball through a maze of lawn chairs set up around the yard. You can time how long it takes to go through your course. Then, challenge a friend to try the course!

Hit the Hoops

Heads up! Don't bother going to the gym to play basketball. You can hit the court right at home!

What You'll Need:
Garbage can or cardboard box, lawn chair, basketball

LOOK OUT, Michael Jordan... here I come! First, you'll have to decide where you want to put your basketball court. If your backyard isn't very flat or a ball doesn't bounce well on it, head to the driveway and get your home court ready to go. Find an empty garbage can or a medium-sized cardboard box and place it up on a lawn chair. That'll be your net. Now you're all set to play some b-ball!

You know the rules: you can dribble (or bounce) the basketball, shoot at your net, and even slam-dunk if you like. But traveling (taking more than two steps without dribbling the ball first) is a no-no. If you're really up for a challenge, place another basket at the opposite end of the drive-way. Now you can play from end-to-end. You can even get a few friends together and play in teams.

You're It!

You've probably played tag tons of times. Why not spice it up?

What You'll Need:
Friends

TAG CAN BE FUN, but try air tag or shadow tag with your friends for something different. In air tag, the only time you're safe is when your feet aren't touching the ground. So if you're being chased, hang from a tree, jump onto a rock, or stand on your hands. Just grab some air! (Lying on the ground with your feet in the air is *not* allowed.) As for shadow tag, the only way you'll become "it" is if your shadow is tagged. So make sure you and your shadow keep on moving!

Bowl-A-Rama

No need to wear rented shoes at this bowling alley. Just set up some pins in your backyard and give it your best shot!

What You'll Need:
Six two-liter plastic bottles, water, softball

LET THE GAMES BEGIN! Find six empty two-liter plastic bottles and pour water into each one until they're nearly half full. Cap the bottles, and there you have it—instant bowling pins! Stand the pins up in front of a wall or fence. Then arrange them into three rows—one row with one bottle, the next with two, and the last with three. Now grab a softball and stand about 15 steps away from the pins. Roll the softball toward the pins and take your best shot. How many bottles can you knock over with one ball? How many tries does it take you to knock them all over? You can challenge a friend to a game of bowling, too. See who can knock over all of the bottles using the fewest balls.

Going Solo

So you wanna play catch but no one's around? No problem! All you really need are two hands and a lot of energy!

What You'll Need:
Rope or net, tennis ball

IF YOU THINK you can't play catch all by yourself, think again. You can...but you've got to be speedy! Tie a net or rope onto two objects, so that you're able to get underneath it easily. Now comes the fun part! Stand on one side of the net and use your left hand to throw the tennis ball up and over the net. Then as quick as a flash, zip under the net and try to catch the ball with your right hand. If you catch it, stay in the spot where you caught the ball and throw it back over the net with the same hand. Now you'll have to catch it on the other side of the net with your left hand. Continue the game and keep score for each hand. Which of your hands makes it to ten points first?

Right on Target

Ready, aim, splash! Do you have what it takes to hit the bull's eye?

What You'll Need:
Clean and empty dishwashing soap bottle, water, empty cans, paper (optional), safe scissors (optional), muffin tin (optional), markers (optional), pennies (optional)

HERE'S A CHANCE to test your aim. But before you can begin target practice, make your official squeeze shooter by filling a soap bottle with water. Now set up the empty cans where it's okay to blast lots of water. Stand about ten to 15 steps away from the cans. Then shoot the water and try to knock them over. If you're up for more difficult target practice, cut out pieces of paper that'll fit snugly into the bottom of muffin-tin cups. On each piece, write a point value. Some cups can be worth five points, some ten, and a couple can be worth 25. Place the pieces of paper in the cups and lean the muffin tin up against a wall. Grab a handful of pennies and, from ten steps away, try to throw pennies one at a time into the muffin cups. If a penny lands in a cup, you get the number of points shown on the piece of paper in that cup.

Tic-Tac-Toe

Toss aside that pencil and paper and play a game of tic-tac-toe with some help from the great outdoors.

What You'll Need:
Stick, rocks, pinecones

X MARKS THE SPOT! To get started with your game of tic-tac-toe, scratch a game board in the dirt with a stick. Then round up some rocks and pinecones. You and a friend can use them to play tic-tac-toe just like you normally do. Instead of drawing circles and Xs, one of you can use rocks and the other can use pinecones. Just like in a regular game of tic-tac-toe, the first one to get three squares in a row wins. If you'd like, you can also play tic-tac-no. It's played just like the game above, except the object of the game is to try NOT to get three squares in a row.

Hop-Along Wrestling

And in this corner... There are no body slams allowed when you get into the ring for this wrestling match!

What You'll Need:
Partner,
grassy space

DON'T LET THE name fool you. This kind of wrestling is nothing like those wild matches on TV. For *this* match, you'll need to round up a friend. The two of you should find a patch of grass or a lawn to stand on. Face each other and join your right hands just like you would if you were shaking hands. Now each one of you should raise your left foot behind your back and hold it up with your left hand. Once you're in position, it's time to wrestle! Both of you should start pushing and pulling the other person with your right hand. You can hop if you want to. The person who remains standing without letting go of their left foot is the winner. Get ready to rumble!

Fore!

There are no golf clubs or holes in this game. You use a Frisbee™!

What You'll Need:
Frisbee™ flying disc,
open space

INCOMING! When you play Frisbee™ golf, all you need is a flying disc and an open space. Gather friends together and pick out some targets around your yard. They can be anything from a garbage can or a tree to a fence post or a big rock. (Be sure to steer clear of windows and other breakables. The last sound you want to hear is "crash"!)

Decide the order in which you want to hit the targets. Then, one at a time, each player should try to hit the first target with the Frisbee™. If you miss, pick up the disc and throw it again from where it landed until you hit the target. Then move to the next hole. Keep track of how many throws it takes for each player to hit each hole. Once all the targets have been hit, the player with the fewest throws wins the game.

Put 'Er There!

Shake a leg (or maybe it's a hand!) and try this off-beat game.

What You'll Need:
Friends, two pieces
of rope,
eight clothespins

Find a few friends and divide into two teams with an equal number on each side. Lay the pieces of rope on the ground about 15 to 20 steps apart. Each team should divide in half. Half of the team lines up behind one rope and the other half behind the other. Then one person on each team puts a clothespin between each finger on their right hand. (That means each kid will hold four clothespins.)

Now the fun begins! The two kids holding the clothespins run to their team members behind the opposite rope and pass the clothespins to a teammate with a handshake—and they can't use their left hand to help! If a player drops a clothespin, he or she can pick it up but must return to the starting line and begin again. When the next team member has the clothespins between his or her fingers, that player runs to the other rope and passes them to the *next* teammate in line. The first team to pass the clothespins to all its teammates wins—hands down!

Loop the Hoop

Try this loopy hoop game and get all tangled up!

What You'll Need:
Hula hoop,
stopwatch or watch
with second hand

If you really want to have some fun with this game, round up as many friends as you can find. Stand in a circle and hold hands. Now comes the loopy part! The object is to pass the hula hoop around the circle. But it's not as easy as it sounds, because you can't let go of each others' hands. When you begin, the hoop should dangle from one player's arm. To move the hoop around the circle, that player will have to step through it and slide it along his (or her) other arm to the *next* player's arm. Continue until the hoop has gone around the whole circle. Watch those feet, arms, shoulders, and heads!

It's in the Bag

Sleeping bags are comfy to sleep in—and great to *race* in!

What You'll Need:
Two pieces of rope, two sleeping bags

ARE YOU READY to race? First, lay the two pieces of rope on the ground so that they're about 15 to 20 steps apart. Then get a few of your friends together and form two equal-numbered teams. Half of each team should stand behind one piece of rope and the other half should stand behind the other. To get started, have one player from each team get into a sleeping bag. On the count of three, the two players in sleeping bags should hop to the other rope. When they pass that rope, the player gets out of the sleeping bag as fast as possible and another teammate hops in. The race continues until everyone on the team has had a turn. The team finishing first is the winner. Get hopping!

Bent Out of Shape

You won't see this race in the Olympics, but it's a lot of laughs!

What You'll Need:
Two pieces of rope, partner

THE RACE IS ON! Lay the pieces of rope on the ground about 15 to 20 steps apart. Now find a friend (or a few) and stand side by side behind one of the pieces of rope. Each of you should spread your feet apart, bend over, and grab your ankles. Now here's the tricky part (and the part where you look a little silly)! You must stay in this position, keeping your knees locked, and walk as fast as you can to the finish line. The one to get there first wins. If you lose your grip or fall over, you have to return to the starting line and begin again. Ready, set, go!

Football Measure-Up

How close can you come to your NFL heroes' personal bests?

What You'll Need:

NFL record book
(from the library),
football,
tape measure,
paper, pen

ARE YOU A JOCK? A sports fiend? A football wannabe? Then maybe it's time to see how you measure up to the pros. Pick your strongest football talent. It could be kicking off, passing, blocking, running, field goals, or any other part of the game. Now take your best shot and measure the distance that you run, toss, or kick. Keep notes and compare them with how the professionals do. Don't expect to be John Elway; it took him years and years of practice to snag back-to-back Super Bowl wins. But Elway will tell you that if you keep doing your best, you're already on your way to some championship moves.

Bubble Trouble

How long can you and your friends keep a bubble going strong before it pops?

What You'll Need:

Socks or wool
gloves,
bubble mixture

ROUND AND ROUND the bubble goes, where it stops, no one knows! Gather some of your friends together and make two equal-numbered teams. Each of you should put a sock or a wool glove over one of your hands. Both teams should form their own circle. Now have one player on each team blow a bubble and hold it in the hand with the sock or glove on it.

If you think that's tough, you ain't seen nothin' yet! This player must pass the bubble to the next player in the circle without popping it. (You should probably play this game when there isn't much wind; otherwise, your bubbles may blow away.) Continue around the circle. The team that passes the bubble all the way around the circle without bursting it is the winner! Don't blow it!

Frisbee™ Fun

Roll out the Frisbee™ for a new spin on soccer, basketball, and football!

What You'll Need:
Two pieces of rope (each around twenty inches long), Frisbee™ flying disc, players

THIS GAME IS a little of this and a little of that! First, place each piece of rope on the ground at opposite ends of your backyard. These ropes will be the nets. Split into two equal-numbered teams. The object of the game is to score a goal in the opposite team's net. You can do this by rolling or throwing the Frisbee™ directly over their rope.

There are a few rules to keep in mind. The player holding the Frisbee™ cannot run with it. The only way to move the Frisbee™ is to throw it to a teammate or roll it on the ground. But if a player on the opposite team grabs the Frisbee™ after it's been thrown, that player gets possession of it. This player can take up to two steps before passing the Frisbee™ to a teammate. The first team with ten points wins. Are you ready to roll?

Baseball Rules!

Answering questions can help beef up your game.

What You'll Need:
Baseball diamond, rule and trivia books, players

NEXT TIME YOUR team needs a little practice AND a little update on basic rules, try this exercise on for size. Instead of swinging the bat for base hits, answer a baseball rule or trivia question instead. There are loads of great trivia books and rule books that you can check out at the public library, so boning up doesn't need to cost a cent. If you get a question right, go to first base and wait for your teammates to bring you home by answering their questions. Knowing who did what, when, and how, and knowing the rules, can only improve your game.

Sardines

No, you don't have to chow down on li'l fishies to win this fun-filled game. It's a new twist on hide-and-seek!

What You'll Need:
Friends

READY OR NOT, here I come! For this game of hide-and-seek, you'll need at least four friends. To get started, one player should be given a chance to hide. The other players should spread out and try to find the pal in hiding. Here's where the twist comes in! When a player finds the pal's hiding place, he or she must hide with that player. Both players must stay where they are until another player finds them. Then that player hides there, too. The hide-and-seek fun will continue until the last person finally finds everybody. At that point, you'll be squished like—you guessed it—sardines!

Don't Back Down

Step right up! Here's a game that proves that standing up isn't always as easy as you think.

What You'll Need:
Friend,
grassy space

TAKE A STAND and challenge your friend to a game that's a lot tougher than it looks. You and your pal should sit back-to-back on a patch of soft grass with your arms folded in front of you. Now each of you should try to stand up without using your arms to help. To do this, you'll have to push yourself up against your friend's back—without losing contact! Do you have what it takes to be the first one to stand up?

Soccey

Mix and match your favorite games.

What You'll Need:
Playing field,
soccer ball,
hockey sticks,
other players

Do you LOVE both hockey and soccer? Then why not mix them up for a fun new adventure? The next time you're dying to move that soccer ball down the field, do it with hockey sticks instead of your agile, soccer-trained feet. The next time you want to slam that puck into the net, slam a soccer ball instead. It's challenging to try and balance out the rules, but the change of pace will be fun and will help you appreciate the wonder of each individual game. Just be careful not to "stick" your fellow players when you're trying to move the ball down the field. It's a game, not a way to collect other people's teeth.

Shoot the Shoebox 🍃🍃🍃

Invite your friends to try their skills at this ingenious game.

What You'll Need:
Hard, smooth
playing surface,
shooter marbles,
shoebox, safe
scissors, pen or
marker, chalk

You MAY HAVE seen skee ball, where players bowl wooden balls up a ramp, at an arcade. Shoot the Shoebox is similar, but relies on skill, not luck. Turn an empty shoebox over and mark various-sized holes on one long edge. One hole should be just big enough for a shooter to go through. Another should be so large that it would be hard to miss. Make the rest of the holes various sizes in between. Cut out the holes with scissors and mark points over them. The largest hole should score zero points. The smallest should have the highest point value. Set the box upside down on a hard surface. Chalk-mark a shooting line five feet away (more for skilled shooters). Each player gets ten shots at the box. If a marble passes through a hole, the shooter gets the number of points marked over it. The player with the most points wins.

Basketball Bundle

This rag-tag replacement will score a few laughs.

What You'll Need:
Basketball court,
bundle of old
clothing,
string,
at least one
other player

IMAGINE YOU'RE MICHAEL JORDAN. You grab the ball and head down center court. You're dying to make that famous "Air" Jordan dunk. Then you realize the "ball" you've palmed won't even bounce. This time, you're playing basketball bundle, and your ball is a well-tied lump of old rags. No fear of double dribbling during this game. No traveling is possible when the ball won't bounce. So just carry, kick, or throw the bundle down the court, shoot and—hopefully—score. Then be glad that rags aren't part of the ordinary NBA plan.

Kick the Can

Your parents or grandparents may have played this as kids!

What You'll Need:
Playing area with
open spaces and
hiding places, at
least three players,
an empty tin can

EVERYONE STANDS on a line in a big space. One person is "it." Another player kicks the can as far as possible. While "it" retrieves the can, everyone else hides. "It" lays the can on the starting line and hunts for other players. Players may change hiding places at any time. What happens when "it" spots a player depends on the version you play. Play continues as long as everyone has fun or until it's dinnertime!

VERSION 1: This version is best for players of different ages and speeds. When "it" finds a player, he or she calls out the name and location of the player. That person immediately goes to jail. "It" continues looking for players. Players can be released from jail if another player sneaks over to the can and kicks it before being spotted by "it."

VERSION 2: If all players have equal speed and agility, alter the rules so that "it" must *tag* a player before the player is jailed. While "it" is chasing, any other player may kick the can to free everyone else from jail.

Backwards Baseball

3, 2, 1—You're out!

What You'll Need:
Playing field, bat, ball, gloves, players

BASEBALL, the Great American Pastime, would be a much tougher game if you had to round the bases and toss the balls backward in order to score or get the other player out. Tougher, yes, but also full of laughs. So the next time you're bored with the traditional game, try this backward twist. You may never look at baseball in quite the same way again. One word of caution: BE CAREFUL WHEN YOU RUN BACKWARD. No game is worth going home injured.

Balloon Paddle Ball

A make-it-yourself active game for indoors or out!

What You'll Need:
Wire coat hangers, old nylon stockings, masking tape or electrician's tape, safe scissors, string, balloons

THESE ARE GREAT outdoor games for a windless day—and are also great for the indoors, because they're easy on the furniture! Make as many rackets as there are players. Carefully pull a coat hanger into a diamond shape with the hook at one corner. Bend the hook into a handle and cover with masking tape. Cut the foot off of an old nylon stocking. Tie the end shut with string. Slip the stocking over the hanger. Tie off around the handle and cut away the excess stocking.

KEEP IT UP: This is a cooperative game for two to four players. Define the boundaries that players must keep their feet inside, then toss a balloon in the air. Keep the balloon up, striking it only with the rackets.

KEEP-AWAY: One person is "it" and stands in the middle of the playing space. All other players keep the balloon in the air and away from "it." If "it" hits the balloon, the person who hit it last becomes "it." If the balloon falls, the person who missed striking the balloon is "it." If the miss was caused by a wild hit, the person who hit the balloon is "it."

Running Bases

Try not to get caught!

What You'll Need:
Grass field, objects to serve as bases, small rubber ball, players

SET UP TWO bases on a patch of grass about 30 feet apart. Two of the players are fielders, each covering one base, and the others are runners. The object is for the runners to move from base to base without being tagged as the fielders toss the ball back and forth in an attempt to lure the runners off base. If a runner is touching a base, he or she is safe, but runners can't just hug the base—they must run at least every second time that the ball is thrown by a fielder. Any player tagged becomes a fielder, and the fielder who tagged the runner out now gets to run the bases!

Sidewalk Sports Crosswords

Line up a few sports terms just for fun.

What You'll Need:
Two colors of chalk, sidewalk

Do you know your sports jargon? The terms for your favorite games? Prove it with this fun sidewalk game of sporty words. The first player writes a sports term horizontally across the sidewalk in one color of chalk. The second must spell a second word, vertically, using one letter from the horizontal word and a different color of chalk. The person with the most words after ten minutes wins. But remember, all of your words have to have something to do with well-known sports. You've got to know your "jock" vocabulary if you want to win this game.

Flashlight Tag

The fun doesn't have to stop when the sun goes down.

What You'll Need:
At least three players, flashlights (optional)

BEFORE PLAYING, check your playing area for any obstacles that could be dangerous. If you can't remove a hazard, mark it with an extra flashlight. Choose one person to be "it" and give that person a flashlight. All other players run and hide. "It" counts to twenty, looks for other players, and "tags" them with a beam of light. Since this kind of tagging can't be felt, players must take "it"'s word when they've been tagged. Tagged players go to a jail, such as a well-lit porch.

Players may change hiding places at any time. Part of the fun is that the darkness provides so many hiding places and makes it easier to sneak from one place to another. Be creative when you search for places to hide. Sometimes all you need is a very dark shadow to conceal you.

A VARIATION: Give all players flashlights. Players can run around or hide as they choose, but must flash their light every time "it" yells "Lights!" Players can also be required to blink their light every ten seconds.

Badminton Bounce

What goes up, must come down... and down... and down.

What You'll Need:
Badminton racquet and birdie, paper, pen

WHEN YOU PLAY badminton, the object is to slam the birdie over the net. But in this game, bouncing the little rubber-tipped cone off your racquet again and again and again can help improve your hand-to-eye coordination and learn just what makes the little birdie fly. You don't even need a net. Toss the birdie into the air. Then "catch" the down-falling cone on the heart of your upturned racquet. See how many times you can bounce the birdie without letting it fall. Keep track of your record and see if you can beat it every time you play.

Hopscotch

This game is a simple way to pass the time alone or with friends.

What You'll Need:
Chalk, rocks or other markers, paved area for playing

Hopscotch in played in some form all over the world. The basics remain the same: Players hop through marked squares without falling. A flat stone called a puck, pottsie, or scotch can mark or claim squares.

Mark the court on a hard surface with chalk. A line of squares should lead up to an end box. Toss the puck into the first space. Jump over the space containing the puck and continue hopping down the court. Always hop on the same foot, except where two squares are side by side. The player must "straddle" these squares, landing with one foot in each square. At the end of the court, turn around and hop back. Losing one's balance is a "miss," and the player leaves the court.

When a player completes the court, the puck is tossed into the next square. Players must always hop over a square with a puck in it, so as more squares are taken up by pucks, it becomes harder. In some versions, players put both feet down to rest in any square that has their own puck in it, but all other players must hop over that square.

Pinecone Pitch

How accurate is your toss?

What You'll Need:
Pinecones, baskets or buckets

The next time your parents ask you to gather fallen pinecones off your lawn (the way you might rake up leaves), make a game of it. Gather as many cones as you can in two large buckets or baskets. Then take turns emptying the baskets and refilling them from 15 paces. See how accurately you can toss the pinecones. How many did you sink? How many missed? Try from different distances. When you're done, you can tell mom and dad that you did your chore—and had fun, too!

Hopping Games

If you like hopscotch, try these games from around the world.

What You'll Need:
Paved area to play, chalk, rocks or other markers

TRY PLAYING HOUSE (or "Real Estate") on any hopscotch court. Each time a player successfully completes the court, he or she tosses the puck over one shoulder. If it lands in a square of the court, the player chalks his or her initials in it. The marked square then belongs to that player and all others must hop over it. The owner of the square uses it as a resting spot. The winner is the player with the most squares.

ENGLISH HOPSCOTCH: Players hold their pucks between their shoes and hop like kangaroos from one large, numbered square to the next. Dropping the puck means the player loses a turn. **SNAIL** is played on a round court with an inside space. Players take turns hopping on one foot from the first space to the center, marked "rest," then back out. Players then toss the puck to get a square, as in "House."

FRENCH HOPSCOTCH: Players perform stunts with the puck while hopping the court. Common stunts include hopping on one foot between squares while kicking the puck to the next square with the hopping foot and balancing the puck on the back of the hand or the toe while hopping.

Boxies

Test your marble-shooting accuracy.

What You'll Need:
Hard, smooth surface, cigar box or cardboard pencil box

HAVE ONE PLAYER hold the box on a hard surface with the lid open. The lid should point at the other players, making a ramp for marbles to roll up. Mark a line five feet from the box (farther for good shooters). Players take turns shooting from the line at the box. Each player gets ten shots. Every marble that rolls up the ramp and drops in the box scores a point. The player with the most points wins.

Gat Fei Gei

Try this Chinese hopscotch game on an airplane-shaped court.

What You'll Need:
Paved area to play, chalk, rocks or other markers

"GAT FEI GEI" TRANSLATES into "Airplane Hopscotch." Mark a court with nine squares in the shape of an airplane, with the "pig's head" at the cockpit. Each player hops on one foot to squares one, two, and three, "straddles" (lands with one foot in each square) four and five, hops on one foot into six, straddles seven and eight, and rests at the pig's head. Then, each player turns and hops back in reverse.

Next, each player stands one by one with toes against square one and tosses a marker at the pig's head. The player hops through the boxes and must retrieve the marker by reaching over one shoulder and bending backwards. Successful players claim square one with their initials.

Now, players step and land on two feet only in their *own* squares. Any player forgetting this rule loses their squares, and other players then compete for them. If the court becomes impossible to play, other players may request a "safe" area in one corner of a chosen square. Only the owner may use the whole square. Once all squares are owned, the pig's head is divided in quarters and players compete for the sections.

Kickball Bouncer

Get a whole new kick out of a tiny soccer ball.

What You'll Need:
Three-inch superball, kickball field, players

KICKBALL GETS A little tricky when the ball you kick and capture is quite small. Don't believe it? Try playing kickball with a tiny, brightly colored three-inch superball. Kicking becomes an art. Covering your base takes a whole new kind of skill. Tagging your opposing team members out isn't nearly as easy as you might think (to avoid painful airborne outs, make sure all tags are done by hand).

Tire Toss

Accuracy counts in this gridiron game.

What You'll Need:
Old tire,
rope,
cinder block,
miniature footballs

READY TO IMPROVE your quarterback accuracy? Shoot for the Big 0. Suspend a tire tied to a rope from a secure tree branch or garage beam (make sure you get your parents' permission before hanging anything from any spot). Get help anchoring the tire at the bottom with something heavy, like a cinder block. Now gather as many small plastic footballs as you can find, step back from the tire about ten paces, and start that rapid-fire passing action. How many balls make it through the circular opening in the tire? The numbers may not be too good when you first start the exercise, but with practice, they'll get better and better. And so will your player-to-player passing accuracy.

Driveway Tennis

Bounce a few—at home.

What You'll Need:
Tennis racquet,
balls,
relatively flat
driveway with
closed garage door

IT'S TOUGH TO make it to the tennis court every day. But if you have a driveway and a smooth garage door, you can bat a few balls between games and work on the strokes you use the most. Stand at the back of your cement driveway, tennis racket and ball in hand. Now drop the ball and hit it on the up bounce toward your CLOSED garage door. When it bounces back to you, pretend the volley came from a skilled competitor sending your best serve back over the net. Don't return the ball too hard, or you'll send it rocketing out into the street. Just use this exercise to streamline your strokes and stay sharp between real matches.

Russia

It takes skill to work your way through this ball-bouncing game!

What You'll Need:
Small rubber bouncing ball, wall with a hard surface underneath, chalk

In RUSSIA, players throw, catch, and do stunts. Mark a chalk line four feet from a high wall. Each player, standing behind the line, in turn throws the ball against the wall, does a stunt, and catches the ball. Anyone missing a level stays there until it is completed.

ONESIES: Throw the ball at the wall and catch it before it hits ground. **TWOSIES:** Throw the ball, let it bounce once between the line and the wall, and catch it. Repeat. **THREESIES:** Throw the ball, clap three times, and catch the ball before it bounces. Repeat three times. **FOURSIES:** Throw the ball, twirl your hands around each other four times, then catch the ball before it bounces. (Four times, and so on.) **FIVESIES:** Throw under one leg and catch it before it bounces. **SIXIES:** Throw the ball behind your back or over one shoulder and catch it before it bounces. **SEVENSIES:** Throw the ball, turn, clap twice, turn again, and catch the ball before it bounces. **EIGHTSIES:** Throw the ball, bring up your right foot and touch your ankle, bring up your left foot and touch your ankle, and catch the ball on the first bounce. **NINESIES:** Throw the ball, spin around, and catch the ball before it hits the ground. **TENSIES:** Bounce the ball seven times on the ground, slap it off the wall with one hand, and catch it before it bounces. Can you do this one ten times?

Four-on-Four

Wide-open hoops.

What You'll Need:
Basketball, court, eight people

FOUR-ON-FOUR basketball tournaments are popping up all over America (the biggest, Hoopfest, happens in Spokane, Washington). Why not try your hand at this fast, challenging version of b-ball? Traditional rules apply. Tournaments use half-courts for a faster, tougher game. But you can play using a full court when you're just starting out.

Pool Games

Games with your friends are twice as much fun in the water!

What You'll Need:
Pool, beach ball or rubber ball, large inner tubes, water guns, brightly painted rocks

If you get to use a swimming pool, you'll probably want to do something more than splash around. Try water basketball! Blow up a large inner tube and find a beach ball or rubber ball that fits through the middle. Divide the players into teams. Players try to shoot the ball through the middle of the moving "hoop." Passing is allowed, and players can swim up to three strokes with the ball in one hand. Players may try to block shots, but are not allowed to push or shove. Some other pool games:

MARCO POLO: "It" closes his or her eyes while the other players spread out in the pool. Every time "it" calls out "Marco!" all the other players must respond "Polo!" "It," eyes still closed, then chases other players and tries to catch them until all players are caught.

TARGET SHOOTING: Set up floating targets like inner tubes, beach balls, or rubber duckies at one end of the pool. Shoot at them with water pistols. Assign points for each target according to difficulty. Allow each player to shoot until the pistol is empty. Score points for each target hit.

Choosing "It"

Have fun even before the game starts!

What You'll Need:
Friends

When you're playing tag or hide-and-seek, you need to pick an "it." To choose one, have every kid kneel in a circle, putting one foot into the center so they all touch at the toes in a smaller circle. Do funny little rhymes like "One potato, two potato, three potato, four, five potato, six potato, seven potato, more!" as you touch a different player's foot, going in the circle, on each syllable. When you get to the word "more!", whoever's foot is touched is "it!" Make up rhymes and silly songs of your own to help choose who becomes "it" next time.

Soccer Just for Kicks

Knock down a few plastic players.

What You'll Need:
Used plastic milk bottles, big field, soccer ball, water (optional)

WANT TO MAKE your soccer kicks count? Try a little target practice. Line up six empty plastic milk bottles at the end of a field, roughly six feet apart. Now, move with your soccer ball from downfield and try to pick off the milk bottles one by one. Try this exercise at rocket speeds. Try it going slow. Try it alone on the field. Try it battling blocks and attempts to steal. Try it with empty milk bottles. Try it with milk bottles filled with water. It's a great way to improve the accuracy of your kicks, even without teammates to help you score.

In and Out

Dodge and dart in and out.

What You'll Need:
Six stationary objects (cones, sandbags), playing field

LEARNING TO TURN on a dime while you run isn't always easy. But swerving in and out of a lineup can help you dodge your opponent's defensive press the next time you play a competitive game. Try this on for size. Arrange six items roughly ten feet apart on a long playing field. The items could be cones, sandbags, backpacks—anything that won't blow away or hurt you if you wind up zigging where you should have zagged. Now run in and out of the line, side to side, at different speeds. Try it at an easy jog. Try it a little faster. Try it at an all-out run. Before you know it, you'll be ready to dodge the defense in *any* game.

 # Toe Tickle Challenge

What can you see with your toes?

What You'll Need:
Blindfold,
five different soft,
rough, or sticky
substances,
bare toes

How MUCH CAN you see with your toes? This fun game will help you find out. Have a friend blindfold you so that you can't see. Now, it's time to tickle your toes. And it's up to you to guess just what tickler your friend has decided to use. Is it a feather? Could it be a slice of juicy orange? Maybe it's the nose of a puppy. It's up to you to use your other senses to try and figure it out. Once your turn is complete, return the favor with your friend blindfolded.

 # String It Along

Play your cards right and you'll win.

What You'll Need:
Ten-foot lengths
of string, staplers,
old playing cards,
friends

THINK YOU'RE READY to win at cards? This game could really string you along. To win this crazy relay, your team has to staple 20 cards to a ten-foot length of string, two cards (one player) at a time. Line up at least 30 feet from the ten-foot lengths of string and staplers. Be sure each player has one card in each hand. When you shout "Go," one player from each team races to their string, grabs the stapler and starts stapling the cards to the string. Once they've hooked two to the cord, they run back and tag the next players in line, who run up and do the same. The first team to securely attach 20 cards to that ten-foot length of string (so no cards fall off when you wave the string in the air) wins!

Baby Step Boogie

Being a baby was never more fun.

What You'll Need:
CD player,
grassy play area,
friends

THIS FUN RELAY depends on how fast you can walk really slow—in baby steps—before the music ends. Pick your favorite up-tempo CD and play it loud and clear. Now line up with a group of your friends and shout, "go!" The first person to move from the starting line to the finish line of a long, flat playing field wins. But there's a catch. You can't just run or sprint. You have to walk in baby steps (heel-toe, heel-toe) through the grass and to the musical beat to win this crazy race.

Footprint ID

Go toe-to-toe to win this game.

What You'll Need:
Bare feet,
washable tempera
paint,
poster board,
markers

WE'VE ALL SEEN fingerprints. But have you ever heard of footprints as a positive ID? It might not hold up in court, but the team that puts its best foot forward certainly wins this game. Divide into two teams. Each person from each team must run to the team poster board, dip a bare foot in tempera paint, make a good, clean footprint, and label the print with a signature before racing back to the line. The team that completes the task first wins. But be careful when you run back to the line with paint on your foot. It can be a slippery! For extra fun, see if you can ID your friends' feet without checking out the names.

Color Collection

You'll need a partner and a timer to really get wild with this game. But it's a test of mental agility you won't be able to resist.

What You'll Need:
Chalk, sidewalk, egg timer, stopwatch, or watch with second hand

SIT OUTSIDE on a sidewalk with a friend. Make sure you each have a piece of chalk. Set the timer for one minute—no more, no less. As soon as you say "go," start searching for as many colors as you can find. Anything in plain sight counts, from tree bark (brown) to hubcaps (silver). The player that lists the most colors on the sidewalk wins.

Stack It Up!

How many pinecones can you stack without watching them fall?

What You'll Need:
Anything stackable you can find outdoors, paper, pen

START OUT STACKING something easy, like leaves or flat rocks. Then, work your way up to tougher hurdles like tree branches or pebbles. Anything you can stack is fair game. Just for fun, keep records of how much of each item you were able to stack.

Alpha Jump Rope

Hop to It!

What You'll Need:
Players, jump ropes (one for each player)

CHOOSE A SUBJECT such as animals, flowers, names, or fruit. As you all jump rope together, each one of you in turn has to name a member of that group alphabetically (for instance, apple, grape, orange, pear) on every second hop. If anyone misses while jumping or can't come up with another item, just start over!

Scent From Above

Experience the sweet smell of success!

What You'll Need:
Strong-smelling items (perfume, oranges, salt, dirty socks), blindfold, paper, pencil or pen

SOME EXPERTS BELIEVE scent is the strongest of human senses. Test the theory with this nosey game. Blindfold each contestant when it is his or her turn. Give the contestant 30 seconds to identify as many objects as possible based on scent alone. Keep track on paper of what the players are smelling and what they guess the object might be. The person to successfully guess the most scents after everyone has had a turn wins the game. Be sure to have plenty of smelly items on hand so everyone has a distinctive new challenge.

Storyteller Scavenger Hunt

Most of us have gone on a scavenger hunt—a race to find items on a list. But this one has a very creative twist.

What You'll Need:
Paper bags for collecting items, friends

EACH TEAM (two or more to a team) must bring back the items on the list (a list like something red, something living, something old, something hard, something soft, something gross). But here's the trick. The winner isn't the one who finds all the items. The winner is the team that finds the items AND comes up with the best story to string them all together.

FOR EXAMPLE: "Once upon a time, a pioneer girl snagged her red hair ribbon on this old piece of barbed wire, while running from a swarm of pill bugs with runny noses. Why were the pill bugs swarming? To steal her bag of marshmallows, of course. They were tired of sleeping on hard, hard stones." Get the picture? This one is bound to be a laugh magnet.

Tree Tag

Tag turns over a new "leaf" with this crazy adaptation.

What You'll Need:
Open space with trees,
packing tape,
blank paper,
markers,
string

IT STARTS OUT normal enough. One person is "it" while the others scatter and run. But there are three to five tree bases, and each runner can only claim sanctuary twice at each tree before they're left with no choice but to run until they're caught.

Clearly mark each tree base with a numbered paper and one blank sheet of paper. Attach them with packing tape so you don't hurt the tree and so it can be easily removed when the game is over. Now give each runner a different colored marker tied to a string around their neck. When they get to the base, they must mark the blank sheet with their color-coded "X." Two strikes, and that tree is not longer a free zone. The last player out wins and can either be "it" or pick the next "it."

By the Number

Hopscotch has always been a game of numbers.
Now it's also a game of observation.

What You'll Need:
Chalk,
pebbles

MAKE A TRADITIONAL hopscotch course. If you want to hop from one numbered square to the next, you'll have to spot something visible in the neighborhood that represents that number. Want to hop to one? Find something solo like a flagpole or a ball. Want to take the leap to two? Find something with two legs or two wheels. Ready to skip over to four? A car with four tires or a dog with four legs had better be nearby. The first one to the last square wins. Use the pebbles to mark your place while someone else takes a turn.

Tree Branch Golf

Your own driving range.

What You'll Need:
Yard,
large, sturdy stick,
pinecones,
sand

Pros like Tiger Woods use expensive golf clubs to shoot for that hole-in-one. But you can play your own crazy game of golf in the backyard. Use a long, sturdy tree branch (one already broken off on the ground) for your club, a pinecone for your ball, and small piles of sand to represent your golf course holes. Be sure to set up your course using hills and rose bushes as hazards that you want to avoid. Keep track of how many strokes it takes to get from start to finish. And when you play again, see if you improve on your score. Don't forget to scatter the piles of sand once your game is finished.

Rocky Mountains

If you have old sidewalks in your neighborhood, try playing this challenging marbles game!

What You'll Need:
Rough sidewalk,
shooter marbles,
small marble,
wrapped candy, or
other prize

Find the roughest, most uneven section of sidewalk that you can. Deep cracks, protruding separators, and blocks lifted by tree roots are all good for testing shooting skill. Set a marble, a piece of wrapped candy, or another small prize in the middle of one sidewalk square. Players kneel on a line two squares from the target and shoot. Depending on the sidewalk's condition, players may have to hit the target in one shot from the line or do it in two or three "strokes." The first person hitting the prize keeps it. Players may then shoot at another prize.

Spelling Bee Baseball

Hit a home run with words.

What You'll Need:
Dictionary,
baseball field,
chalk (optional),
pebbles (optional)

Y OU CAN BE a baseball All-Star even if you can't hit, pitch, or throw. Because in this version of the game, you round the bases just by spelling words correctly. It's your pitcher's job to toss out tough (but not impossible) words. It's the batter's job to take a swing at spelling the word right. And it's up to your umpire to check the spellings in the dictionary. Just like in regular baseball, if you miss three times in a row, you're out. Three outs, and the other team is up. Don't feel like physically rounding the bases? Draw a baseball diamond on the side-walk and use pebbles as players.

Swing the Statue

Here's an easy game that will exercise your imagination!

What You'll Need:
Open playing area
with soft surface,
three or more
players

P LAY THIS GAME on grass or sand; it involves falling down. One player, chosen as "it," takes each player by the hand one at a time and swings them in a circle. When "it" lets go, the player stays frozen in whatever position he or she lands in. When all players are swung and released, "it" becomes an art critic, walking among the statues and "critiquing" each one. The "statues" must stay frozen—no smiling or laughing! If the statue fails to freeze, he or she is out. The ones who stay statuesque are the winners. Choose a new "it" for the next round.

A VARIATION: After "it" swings all the statues, he or she chooses a category, such as zoo animals, cartoons, kitchen tools, or famous people. Players must remain in their positions, but may move any arm or leg they're not using to support their weight to try and resemble something in that category.

Sidewalk Tennis

323

Often called box ball, this tennis doesn't need expensive rackets!

What You'll Need:
Two players, level sidewalk, small bouncing ball

Choose two large sidewalk squares as your court. Only the ball can enter the court; players must keep their feet out. The center line between the two squares splits the court in two (as a net). Players stand at the edge of their squares. One player serves by bouncing the ball and striking it with an open hand. The ball should bounce once in the opposite player's square. The opposite player then hits the ball so it bounces once in the server's square. If a player misses, the opponent gets a point. The first to reach 21 wins. In some versions, the game continues past 21 until someone scores *two* more points than their opponent.

Knucklebones

324

Try these ancient jacks and dice games!

What You'll Need:
Five pebbles or small knucklebones

Knucklebones are small, almost cubic bones from an area in an animal's legs equivalent to our wrists and ankles. Children in ancient times saved these bones for play. Even adults saved the bones and played dice games with them. If you can't find *real* knucklebones, find five round pebbles each a half to three-quarters of an inch across.

PICKUPS: Drop four bones on a flat surface in front of you. Save the fifth, called the "jack." In the first round, toss the jack in the air, snatch up one bone while the jack is still in the air, and catch the jack on the way down. Move the bone to your other hand, and try again for the next bone. If you catch all four bones without missing the jack, toss the bones out again for a second round. In the second round, you must snatch *two* bones before catching the jack. In the third round, you grab three bones and the lone bone. In the fourth round, you grab all four bones. If you miss the jack, your opponent takes a turn.

Gymnastics Jam

Excel at your own Olympic events.

What You'll Need:
Flat, open field of grass, sidewalk, chalk, 3x5 notecards, pens or pencils

ONE OF THE MOST popular Olympic events is gymnastics. From the balance beam to the uneven parallel bars to the rings to the wide-open floor exercise events, gymnasts are amazing. You can't learn those remarkable skills overnight. But you can adapt some events to create your own gymnastics jam. Draw a make-believe balance beam on your sidewalk with chalk. The make up silly steps, hops and twirls, somersault your way across a grassy field, and dangle from your swingset rings. Then have your friends score your routines by holding up numbered cards from one to ten. Take turns being an athlete and a judge.

Black Snake

Play this fun game of marble golf.

What You'll Need:
One marble for each player (shooter size), dirt playing area, paper, pencil or pen

USE THE HEEL of your shoe to scoop out a long row of shallow holes in the dirt. The distance between holes should be about twice the distance the average player can shoot. Make nine or ten holes. Each player shoots from a line drawn n the dirt near the first hole. Players take turns shooting, one hole at a time. The object is to shoot the marble into each hole. The marble must fall into hole one before you can shoot for hole two. Keep track of how long it takes to complete the course. The person who completes the course in the fewest shots wins. To make the game even more challenging, each person who completes the course can be a "black snake" who can shoot his or her marble at the other players' marbles, knocking them off course.

Beanbag Volley

No more sore fingers!

What You'll Need:
Beanbags or bean-filled stuffed animals, volleyball net

Millions of Americans love playing volleyball. But the hard surface of the ball can be tough on young fingers and fists. So why not volley one of your favorite beanbag-stuffed animals instead of that hard-to-handle ball? Adapt the rules a little to allow for the fact that the beanbag won't always "bounce" as high as the ball would. Make it legal to toss the stuffy overhand, as long as it's not held for more than three seconds. Then have fun!

Trailblazing

Try this cool variation of hide-and-seek.

What You'll Need:
Three or more players, an outdoor area with hiding places, chalk or sticks for each player

Begin by choosing an "it." Have "it" close his or her eyes (or stand where other players can't be seen) for a specific length of time. The rest of the players run off in the same direction to find hiding places, but must mark their paths by chalking arrows on paved areas or placing arrows made of sticks on the ground. Marks should be several yards apart. When the players reach a good hiding place, they leave arrows pointing in four different directions. At this point the players scatter and find hiding places within twenty paces of the mark. "It" follows the trail and tries to find all the players.

In a more active version, called "Hares and Hounds," players divide into two teams. The "hounds" close their eyes while the "hares" run together in a particular direction, leaving chalk marks or stick arrows along the way. After a ten- or 20-second head start, the hounds chase the hares. The round is over when the hounds spot the hares. The hares must lay trail markers at least every ten yards.

Predator and Prey

How good a predator can you be? Find out by playing this game.

What You'll Need:
Three or more players, outdoor area with plenty of hiding places

PREDATORS MUST BE good at hiding to sneak up on their prey. If prey animals want to avoid being caught, they must use their senses to detect predators. Many prey species stay in open areas where it's hard for predators to sneak up. To simulate this natural relationship, have one person be the prey animal. With closed eyes, the prey counts to twenty while the predators hide. Every predator must find a separate hiding place from which he or she can see the prey *but cannot be seen* by the prey. Predators may be close or far away as long as they stay within agreed-upon boundaries.

When the prey finishes counting, he or she may begin looking, and may lean in any direction, but cannot leave the starting spot. Predators may change hiding places at any time, but must stay where they can see prey at all times. If the prey spots a predator, he or she calls out the name of that person, who is out and must come back to base. When the prey has spotted all predators, choose a new prey.

Jump Rope Relay

Race to the finish with a hoppy attitude.

What You'll Need:
Two jump ropes, open space with asphalt blacktop, a "base"

TO SPEED UP both your rope skipping skills and your agility, try on this hopp-enin' relay for size. Line up in two teams at the starting line of a blacktop playground. When the starter says "go," begin jumping rope down the blacktop. When you get to the base you've set up on the other end of the blacktop, tag the base, skip back to the starting line, and tag the next racer. The team to finish the race first wins.

Categories

Test your mind and your balance with this chalked-court game.

What You'll Need:
Hard surface, chalk, rocks or other markers, small bouncing ball

THIS CHALLENGING GAME will teach you to think fast! Mark off a court in the style of a hopscotch court. In each square, write the name of a category—for example, cars, fruits, birds. Players place their markers in the first square. Each player in turn walks or hops through the squares, bouncing the ball and naming something from the first category for each step in each square. Ball, foot, and word must arrive at the same time. No word can be used twice in any one run of the court. Players who finish the court place their markers in the next square and must name things from *that* category. The first player to finish all categories wins and chooses the categories for the next game.

AN ALPHABET VARIATION: Each time a player steps in a square, he or she must name something from the category in that square, all items named starting with the same letter. A player faced with the categories of cars, fruits, and birds might say, "Buick, blackberry, blue jay."

Hit the Coin

Games don't need to be complicated to be fun!

What You'll Need:
Two players, sidewalk, any coin or token, small bouncing ball

FIND A LEVEL SIDEWALK of large concrete squares. Place a coin or some other token on the seam between two squares. Each player stands on the other ends of the concrete squares with their toes on the seam so that each is one square from the coin. (If the squares are small, players can move two squares away.) The object is to hit the coin with the ball and move it into the opponent's square. Each direct hit scores one point. Flipping the coin scores two points. The first to reach 21 points wins the game. In some versions, the player also wins the coin.

Ringer

Learn to play the most common marbles game.

What You'll Need:
Hard, smooth playing surface, chalk, regular-sized playing marbles, larger "shooter" marble for each player

WHEN WE THINK of marbles, we usually think of some variation of Ringer (also called Taw, Ring Taw, Circle, and Big Ring). In some areas kids join leagues and play in tournaments. You don't have to be on a team, though, to enjoy the game. Mark a large circle on a hard, smooth surface. Draw your circle any size. Set nine to 13 marbles in the center in a cross. The marbles should each be an inch or two apart.

One player kneels by the circle and grips the shooter with one hand, knuckle down behind the circle's outline. With a flick of the thumb, the player sends the shooter into the marbles in the ring. A player who knocks a marble from the ring keeps the small marble and shoots again. The player continues shooting until he or she fails to knock a marble out, and the next player takes a turn. If the shooter accidentally falls from the player's hand while trying to shoot, the player can call "slips" and try again—but only if no marbles in the ring have been touched. When all the marbles are knocked out, the player with the most wins the game. In "keepsies," the players win the marbles, too!

Leaf, Leaf, Pinecone

A new version of an old circle game.

What You'll Need:
Pine cone, friends, grassy circle

THIS NEW VERSION of "Duck, Duck, Goose" has a nature-friendly twist. Whoever is "it" must not only touch the heads of the other players, saying, "Leaf, leaf, leaf," but must also drop a big, fresh pinecone in the lap of the victim they choose before running back around the circle without being tagged. The person trying to tag "it" can touch "it" with a hand above the waist or with the pinecone below the waist.

Really BIG Handball

Get a big start on a little game.

What You'll Need:
Play ball,
outdoor handball
court

IT'S NOT EASY to master handball when you're a kid. The ball is so small and the sport is so fast. So why not start out playing really BIG? Bat around your favorite colorful play ball until you get the feel of the court and the rhythm of bouncing the ball off the wall and waiting for your partner to return that "serve." In addition, a big soft ball will hurt a lot less than a tiny, rock-hard sphere when it gets away and lands square on the side of your head.

Jumpin' With Jacks!

Here's your chance to learn how to use jacks.

What You'll Need:
Jacks set with
rubber ball,
hard surface for
playing

JACKS COMES FROM ancient games in which one object was tossed in the air and other objects were picked up before the player caught the "jack" on the way down. To play, toss metal jacks on a hard surface. They should scatter, but none should be out of reach. Bounce the ball once on the ground and snatch one piece. Catch the ball in the same hand before it strikes the ground again. Move the metal piece to the other hand and continue until you catch all the pieces without dropping the ball. If you miss, begin again. This is "onesies."

Now, bounce the ball and snatch up the pieces two at a time before you catch the ball. This is "twosies." Stay at twosies until you get all the pieces. In "threesies," pick up the pieces three at a time, in "foursies," four at a time, and so on, until you pick up all the pieces at once.

If you play with others, player one picks up jacks until he or she misses. Player two then takes a turn.

In Your Neighborhood

How well do you know your own neighborhood? Who lives next door? What is there to do at the playground? What kinds of trees are around your house? How clean is the water in your community? The activities in this chapter will help you discover what your neighborhood has to offer. You might be inspired to start a local improvement project to make your living space look nicer, or to join a Neighborhood Watch program to keep your area safe.

Rockin' Paint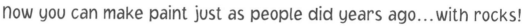

Now you can make paint just as people did years ago…with rocks!

What You'll Need:
Safety goggles, crumbly rocks, charcoal, soil, clay, some big rocks, old bowl, cornstarch or corn syrup, water, paintbrush, paper

FORGET ROCK 'N' ROLL. It's time to rock 'n' paint! Make your own paint with materials like rocks, charcoal, soil, and clay. First, put on your safety goggles to protect your eyes. Then, gather crumbly rocks, charcoal, heavy pieces of soil, and clay on a big rock and use another rock to crush them into a fine powder. (Watch your fingers!) Believe it or not, this powder will be the base for your paint. Mix the powder in a bowl with a little cornstarch and water (or just some corn syrup) to make a paste-like mixture. Now you're ready to create a masterpiece with your own homemade paint! Just dip a brush into the mixture and get to work painting on your paper. Have a look around your backyard and see what other things can be crushed to make paint and what materials don't work all that well. Try things like grass, flowers, leaves, or sticks. Hard rocks won't work too well. See if you can mix different colors that will add some flair to your works of art!

High-Flyin' Fun

It's a bird. It's a plane. Nope…it's a high-flying kite!

What You'll Need:
Two thin sticks
(one of them twice
as long as the other),
string,
tape,
safe scissors,
plastic shopping bag

BUILD YOUR OWN kite and head for the sky! Find two sticks and place them together so they look like a small "t." Using string, tie the sticks together where they overlap. Next, form a diamond shape around the outside of the sticks with some more string. As you do this, wrap the string around the ends of each stick a few times and tape the string tightly in place as well. This is the frame of your kite.

Now, cut a plastic shopping bag at its seams so that you have a completely flat piece of plastic. Lay the frame on top of the plastic and then cut around it, making sure the plastic is a couple of inches bigger than the frame. Now put the plastic over your frame and tape it in place. Attach the kite string to where the sticks overlap. And just like that, you're up, up, and away!

Mud Madness

Here's mud in your eye! Getting dirty is the name of the game when it comes to building with mud.

What You'll Need:
Stick,
soil,
flour,
water,
dull knife

WHEN YOU WERE younger, you probably loved to make mud pies. But now you can do more with mud than make a sloppy blob of goo. Using a stick, mix together some soil, flour, and water until it's stiff and looks like dough. Now shape this mixture into a large rectangle (around three feet by two feet—about as big as a sofa cushion) and let it dry until it's firm. Once it's ready, have an adult cut the large brick into small bricks with a dull knife. You can use these bricks to build whatever you can imagine—a building, a city, a space station, or something else entirely. What muddy masterpiece can *you* create?

Rainwater Blues

How clean is the air you breathe? The water you drink? Rain can help you find out.

What You'll Need:
Clean pan or jar,
coffee filter,
second jar or cup

IF YOU'VE EVER wondered what particles slip inside your body from the air you breathe or the water you drink, this is an interesting way to find out. Place a clean jar or pan in an open area just as it starts to rain. Collect as much rain as you can for the first hour of the storm. Now gather the rainwater and carefully pour it through a clean coffee filter, catching the water in a second jar or cup. Peel open the coffee filter and see what the rain washed out of your atmosphere. You might look at breathing in a new way after checking out this environmental strain.

Taking Notice

More power in your kid corner.

What You'll Need:
Notebook,
pen or pencil,
envelope,
stamp

KEEP TRACK OF how your community is doing when it comes to pollution. The next time you and your family jump in the car and head downtown, bring along your enviro-journal and keep your watchful eyes peeled.

Is there garbage on your city streets? Where is the garbage (and what kind of trash did you see)? Do cars around you belch out too much smoke and exhaust? Make a note of that too. Is it easy to breathe the city air? Easy to see down the street? Don't forget to write that down.

Keep track of the environmental details you can see for yourself every time you head for the downtown streets. Then mail copies of those notes to your favorite newspaper or the governor's office. Let them know kids are keeping score, and everyone will win.

Chalk It Up

Add some temporary colorful art to your urban world.

What You'll Need:
nature magazines,
sidewalks or
blacktop,
colored chalk

IF YOU EVER get tired of your urban jungle, take the chalk challenge and brighten your world. Open your favorite nature magazine to a color photograph. Now try to duplicate the brightest, most wonder-filled pictures right in your own front (or back) yard using your own chalk. Do you love the jungle and the monkeys that call it home? Chalk them in swinging across your driveway. Do you dream of colorful tropical birds? Draw them on the sidewalk beyond your front door. It will remind you how lucky you are to be a citizen of this wonderful world.

Operation Neighborhood

When you help, others catch the fever.

What You'll Need:
A few friends,
work gloves,
trash bags,
broom,
dustpan

SOMETIMES ALL IT TAKES is one hero to start a wave of participation. You can be that hero by organizing a group of young volunteers to do a little neighborhood cleanup. Ask your friends if they care about the neighborhood they call home. If, like most kids, they answer "yes," tell them it's time to turn their good thoughts into good deeds.

Get permission from friends and neighbors before you begin, then grab some work gloves and a big trash bag and dig in. Is there a broken-down fence scattered across the alley? Take the time to gather it up and toss it in the trash. Did somebody break glass bottles all over the street? Grab a broom and a dustpan and sweep that mess into the trash. You'll feel like a hero and your streets will reflect how much you care.

Micro-Hike

Take a tiny hike into a tiny world and discover what lives there.

What You'll Need:
String,
safe scissors
short stakes,
magnifying glasses,
paper and
toothpicks (optional)

MEASURE OUT about 20 to 30 feet of string. Tie each end to a short stake, such as a tent stake. Take your string and stakes outdoors and stretch the string across an area with some variation. You might run it across part of a lawn, under an arching shrub, and alongside a flower bed. The string doesn't have to be straight; it can run along the base of a fence or beside a pond or stream. Secure the line with more stakes if necessary. Make sure that you and every person who will be "hiking" with you has a magnifying glass.

Start at one end of the string on your hands and knees. Use your magnifying glass to examine everything under the string. Look for different kinds of plants, including moss between the grass blades or under a shrub. Look for fungi of different forms. Find animals such as insects, spiders, and worms.

Move slowly down the string, searching for every living thing you can find. You might end up taking a whole hour to hike! You never know what interesting things you'll find. When you're done, write down what you've seen or compare your observations with those of others who "hiked" with you. What interesting things did they see that you missed? When you're all done, use paper and toothpicks to make tiny signs to mark the most interesting discoveries. Then invite others to take your hike!

Stream of Consciousness

Clean up America, one stream at a time.

What You'll Need:
Work gloves,
trash bags,
adult supervision

Your LOCAL STREAMS and rivers are valuable natural resources. But they need your help to get rid of unsightly litter. Ask your parents if you can form a kids-only weekend work crew to help put garbage in its place (make sure at least one adult goes along for advice and supervision).

Gather at a different section of stream each weekend for four weeks at a time. Dress in old, grubby clothes and sneakers or boots. Bring garbage bags, work gloves, plenty of fresh water to drink, healthy snacks, and a good attitude. Be sure to search the land near the stream, the banks, and the shallows just off the banks for signs of trash or debris. Carefully gather up trash and put it in large, sturdy trash bags. If you see any dangerous garbage, such as broken glass or hypodermic needles, DO NOT TOUCH. Notify the adult on your team and let him or her decide what to do.

Leave it to Nature

Fall into community composting.

What You'll Need:
Rake,
garbage bags,
telephone

AFTER YOU RAKE and bag your leaves, it's time to pick up the telephone. Call your local city government office and ask if they have a community compost location. If they do, talk mom and dad into loading the leaves into your family car instead of the trash collection barrel. Bring your compost over to the community location and leave it there—allowing nature to break down the organic material and keep trash landfills free for other disposables.

Live Christmas Tree

Make Christmas a year-round activity.

What You'll Need:
Rooted Christmas tree, backyard garden spot, shovel

THEY MAY COST a little more—sometimes a LOT more—but live, rooted Christmas trees are a great way to help reforest Planet Earth AND keep your holiday memories alive. Each year, have your family buy a rooted tree. In the spring, plant this living tribute to your family holiday traditions. In doing so, you make the yard look more beautiful and help the planet process both oxygen and carbon dioxide.

Such a Sap

Plant a seed of hope.

What You'll Need:
Tree seedlings, small shovel

HUNDREDS OF RAINFOREST acres are depleted every year by greedy corporations or by hungry locals trying to make a decent living. Either way, trees are vanishing, and with those trees, the oxygen supply and animal habitat they used to provide are vanishing too.

You can't always stop deforestation in other countries. But you can help rebuild the ecosystem, starting with your own backyard. Buy tiny tree starts or saplings at your local home and garden center, or write to the National Arbor Day Foundation (100 Arbor Ave, Nebraska City, NE, 68410) to buy saplings. The sooner you plant, the sooner we all breathe a little easier.

Sand Sift Saturday

Make being beached good "clean" fun.

What You'll Need:
Rake,
work gloves,
trash bags

EVER NOTICED how much junk winds up in a playground sandbox? For some reason that scientists and philosophers have never discovered, a lot of people think children's sand pits are giant ashtrays or garbage cans. Until we figure out why this happens and how to stop it, make a difference by cleaning up the mess other people leave behind.

Help sift out the icky stuff left behind using an ordinary rake. Once you have a good-sized pile of junk, slip on your work gloves and bag it up. You'll be doing your neighborhood (and the littler kids that look up to you) a big favor. But be especially careful of broken glass and anything that even LOOKS like a needle. If you find *that* type of waste in a sandbox, ask an adult for advice on what to do.

Duck Bread Distribution

Quack, quack, give something back.

What You'll Need:
Old stale bread and
cereal products,
wild ducks

HOW OFTEN HAVE you watched your folks toss out stale or moldy bread and cereal? Well, stop watching and start retrieving. There are hungry ducks to feed! Take those old edibles to the park or duck pond (or wherever your local mallards hang out) and give the fowl a feast. Be sure to throw the boxes and wrappers away before you leave.

Earth Day Parade

Celebrate in style.

What You'll Need:
Bicycles, newspaper streamers, recycled cloth strips, bottle caps, twigs, branches, leaves, pinecones

WHEN EARTH DAY rolls around on April 22, why not gather your friends together and have a recyclers' parade? Decorate your bicycles, your wagons, your dogs, and yourself with newspaper streamers, strips of recycled cloth, bottle cap noisemakers—anything you can string together using recycled goods. Make sure you have your parents take plenty of pictures. Then write to your local newspaper about your private parade. Next year, you might wind up in the newspapers you recycle. Be sure to clean up after you're done.

Paper or Plastic?

Just DO IT!

What You'll Need:
Three recycling bins, the desire to sort

IN THE PAST ten years, Americans have recycled more aluminum, plastic, and paper than ever before. We've even pocketed thousands of dollars for some of our efforts. But we still have a ways to go before we can say we recycle most of our reusable trash.

Ask your folks if you can keep three recycle bins on the back porch near your kitchen. When a plastic bottle is headed for the trash, reroute it to your plastic's recycle bin (don't forget to remove the cap before you do). Do the same for aluminum cans and newspapers. Then call your local city government to find out how to get these goodies to recycling centers. Many towns now offer curbside pickup in the same way they pick up traditional trash.

Neighborhood Theme Walks

353

Take a walk with your family and keep your eyes open for something special!

What You'll Need:
Paper and pencil, coin to flip

FAMILY THEME WALKS are fun. They're a good way to provide the exercise that everyone needs, and a great way to get to know your neighborhood. However, when you walk, there are safety rules to remember. Make sure to stay on the sidewalk or shoulder and don't walk in the street. Be sure you walk on the left-hand side of the road whenever you can, so that you face traffic. Finally, cross the street *only at street corners.* Always look both ways and make sure it is safe to cross. Before you go, decide what theme to use. Here are some ideas:

FIRSTS: Look for the first daffodil of spring, the first rose of summer, the first barbecue cookout on the block.

TALLY IT UP: Tally the houses on your block and see what color is most popular. Do the same with cars. What else can you tally?

ALPHABET WALKS: Look for and name anything you see beginning with a certain letter.

COLOR WALKS: Look for (and name) anything you see of a particular color. Or give each person a card cut from colored paper and have them try to find something that matches it exactly.

COIN-FLIP WALK: At every street corner, flip a coin. If it turns up heads, turn right. If it's tails, turn left. See where you end up after a certain length of time, then reverse your direction and head home.

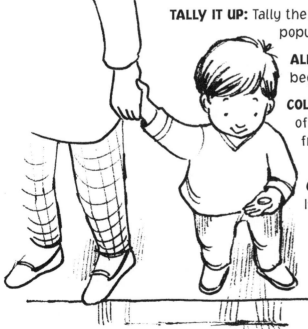

Bike Hike

Take bike hikes with your family and watch your miles add up!

What You'll Need:

Bicycles,
helmet for each rider,
water bottle,
snacks,
notebook,
national or world map,
pushpins,
marker

IF YOUR FAMILY IS into biking, try planning some bike hikes with them. One great incentive to keep everyone biking is to plan an imaginary trip. Find out how far your "destination" is, then see how long it takes you to bike that many miles. When biking, be sure to observe these safety tips:

1) Inspect your bicycle before each ride. Inflate the tires, check the brakes, and lubricate the chain properly.

2) All riders, both adults and children, should wear helmets. Make sure your helmet protects your forehead. Always buckle the straps and make sure they fit snugly.

3) Remember, your bike is a moving vehicle. You must follow the rules of the road. Ride on the right-hand side. Obey all traffic signs and signals, using hand signals to indicate when you turn.

4) Be alert for cars at all times. *Always* assume that the driver doesn't see you. Watch for cars turning at corners or backing out of driveways.

If you're going to be out more than an hour, bring water and snacks. Use a map to plan your route and figure out how many miles you will travel. After a while you'll get pretty good at estimating how far you've biked. After each hike, record your mileage in a notebook. On a wall map, mark your town (and your "destination") with pushpins, then use a colored marker to note on a highway the number of miles you've biked.

See how long it takes you to bike around the country—or the world!

Beautify the Neighborhood

Plan an outdoor cleanup project with family and neighbors.

What You'll Need:
Gardening tools, plenty of helpers

YOU'VE PROBABLY SEEN a spot or two in your area that needs sprucing up. Perhaps the parking strip in front of your own house is full of weeds. Maybe the nearby park looks blah. First, list what to do: get permission, pull weeds, dig up soil, re-seed grass, plant trees, plant flowers. Cross things off your list that are too difficult, expensive, or hard to maintain, and check with your local government before fixing public property. Tell everyone about your idea. See if any neighbors, friends, or local clubs would like to help. Set a date to meet. When everyone is together, dig in! Everyone can help pull weeds. Adults can dig up hard soil and trim shrubs. Children can help plant flowers and small trees.

Scavenger Hunts

Plan a fun hunt to cover the neighborhood or just your block.

What You'll Need:
Paper and pencil, paper bags for small items

GIVE TEAMS of two to four kids a list of ten to 20 things to find. Make sure the items on the list are hard, but not impossible, to find. Items must be collected from public areas or neighbors who give permission. Teams can also "collect" trees or buildings by writing down their locations or by drawing pictures. For a **HALLOWEEN HUNT,** find something green like the face of Frankenstein's monster, something pale like a vampire, or sharp like a werewolf's fang. Spot three stores with Halloween displays in front. Collect ingredients for a witch's cauldron.

ECO-HUNT: Pick up something thrown away that can be recycled. Spot three examples of people helping wildlife. Find a bird's nest (but don't disturb it). Spot three types of flowers used by butterflies or bees.
KNOW YOUR NEIGHBORHOOD: Find the largest tree in the neighborhood, a house with a red door, or the nearest mailbox. List houses with basketball hoops, birdbaths, wishing wells, pink flamingos, or birdhouses.

Clues of the Past

Look for signs of earth-shaping events.

What You'll Need:
A map of your community or a place of special interest

THE SURFACE OF the earth is constantly moving as water and weather erode the rocks and move the soil. You can find evidence of recent geological events—and perhaps ancient events as well! Use a map to explore your community or some other special place. Mark what you find on your map. Floods, for example, leave watermarks on buildings. Also look for scouring of stream banks and for debris in tree branches.

Huge glaciers, which once scoured a large part of the North American continent, left distinctive marks behind. Large, exposed rock faces may have had long scratches cut into them as rocky undersides of glaciers passed over them. If you live in the northern United States, look for areas around your community that are flat and have many small lakes. These areas were scoured out by glaciers. Glaciers also "rafted" large rocks from one area of the country to another. Look for boulders of a kind of rock not normally found in your area.

Around the mountains, look for the same kind of scratches on rock faces that continental glaciers left behind. Also seek what geologists call U-shaped valleys. These are broad valleys cut by glaciers. Valleys cut by streams tend to be V-shaped. Also search for areas where soil has been exposed and eroded by running water. Too much erosion causes stream banks to collapse and can lead to landslides. If you see a very muddy stream, follow it upstream to see if the mud comes from erosion along the banks. Look also for signs of erosion control in your community, such as trees planted on bare slopes.

Billboard Bonanza

How much is too much? You decide.

What You'll Need:
Notebook,
pen,
envelope,
stamp

THE NEXT TIME you go for a walk or a drive in the town or city with your parents, keep track of how many advertising billboards or advertising benches you see (and how far your drive was). Were too many billboards blocking the natural view? Too many ugly advertising messages on pedestrian benches? Keep an accurate record of what you saw and how it made you feel. Send the statistics to the governor of your state (ask your parents to help you find his or her address).

Fishmas Trees

Ho, ho, ho—under the ice.

What You'll Need:
Discarded natural-cut Christmas tree, permission from your local parks department

THE NEXT TIME you buy a live, cut Christmas tree, don't just throw it in the landfill when the ho-ho-hos are over. Rather than waste it, toss the whole tree—branches, needles, and all—on a frozen lake.

Now why would you do that? Well, *you* may be warm and toasty inside your house, but the wildlife in your town might not be. The discarded tree provides a nice windbreak and warm resting place for migrating birds who stop along the way. It even warms the water beneath the ice by several degrees, providing relief for winter-bound fish.

Froghopper

Ribbit, ribbit.

What You'll Need:
Patience,
wetlands

WE ALL KNOW dinosaurs became extinct some 65 million years ago. Many scientists believe the frogs of the world could be next to go. These friendly amphibians seem to be facing the same destiny—just like many big cats of the world. Have the frogs and toads in your region started to vanish? Take an afternoon to find out. Head to your local pond or shoreline and watch for hoppers in shallow water!

Drive-by Fiction

Let your imagination take you on a wild ride.

What You'll Need:
Imagination,
notebook,
pencil or pen

MOST PEOPLE WONDER how writers come up with their stories and tales. This fun activity might give you a pretty good idea. Sit with a friend and a notebook, facing the street. Carefully watch the cars as they drive by, one by one by one. Watch the people walking their dogs or riding their bikes. What are the people wearing? How do they sound? What things are they carrying with them? What do their cars' license plates say? Do their cars run smoothly? Are their cars' windshields cracked? Make as many observations as you can about five different people. Now build a story around those people. Share it with your family, teacher, or friends, or just write it down for fun. But let your imagination run wild!